Living Illustrations

J. B. FOWLER, JR.

Living
Illustrations

BROADMAN PRESS
Nashville, Tennessee

4222-60
ISBN: 0-8054-2260-9

Dewey Decimal Classification: 808.88
Subject Heading: ILLUSTRATIONS
Library of Congress Catalog Card Number: 85-4175

Printed in the United States of America

The illustrations marked with the dagger symbol (†) formerly appeared in *Proclaim* and are used by permission.

Library of Congress Cataloging in Publication Data

Fowler, J. B., 1930-
Living illustrations.

Includes index.
1. Homiletical illustrations.   I. Title.
BV4225.2.F68   1985   251'.08   85-4175
ISBN 0-8054-2260-9

Dedication

This volume is affectionately dedicated to my wife, Wanda, for the encouragement she has given to me in more than thirty years of preaching ministry.

Preface

I am a confirmed believer in the use of illustrations. And I take my inspiration for using them from the Savior Himself about whom it is written: "All these things spake Jesus unto the multitude in parables; and without a parable spake he not unto them" (Matt. 13:34).

The sensitive minister has often observed the hush that falls over a congregation when an illustration is used in a sermon. And the better and more gripping the story, the more the attention is riveted on the speaker.

As I see it, there are no better illustrations available than those that are drawn from literature and history. Each is a living library, teeming with all the emotions of life that bless or distress those to whom we speak. And when those quality illustrations are used skillfully by the speaker, they drive the point home unforgettably and rivet it permanently to the memory.

Solomon, reputed to be the wisest man who ever lived, said that there was nothing new under the sun. And following the wisdom of the sage, I confess that these illustrations are neither new nor original. They have been drawn from sources too numerous to mention even if I could remember them all. And they have been taken directly from sermons I have preached to congregations over the past thirty years.

I humbly acknowledge my indebtedness to those who have contributed their illustrations to my preaching. Thank you, dear friends. If it were possible for me to do so, I would call each of you by name and give you the credit you so richly deserve.

Contents

Age

No matter how old you are, you are not too old to be useful.

Commodore Vanderbilt made hundreds of millions of dollars when he was past seventy. Kant did some of his best philosophical writing when he was past seventy. After he was eighty, Goethe wrote the second part of *Faust*.

Tennyson was eighty-three when he wrote "Crossing the Bar." Benjamin Franklin did his most active work for his country after he was sixty. Viscount Palmerston was elected prime minister of England at seventy-one, and he was reelected at seventy-five. Christy was premier of Italy at seventy-five.

Verdi was writing operas past his eightieth birthday; Titian painted the *Battle of Lepanto* at ninety-eight and his *Last Supper* at ninety-nine; and Michelangelo was still producing sculptural masterpieces at eighty-nine.

You are never too old to live![†]

Angels

Corrie ten Boom related a remarkable experience that took place at Ravensbruck, a Nazi prison camp, when she and her sister were interned there during World War II.

As a large group of women was being processed into the camp, the women guards searched them carefully. Asking if she and her sister might use the bathroom, Corrie and sister Betsie went in to the ladies room, and Carrie told Betsie to take off her woolen underwear. Then Corrie removed her woolen underwear.

Rolling her precious little Bible up in the underwear, she laid the clothing in a corner of the ladies room; and walking back to the line of women, she whispered to her sister that the Lord would answer their prayers and protect their little Bible.

Later, after she and Betsie had showered and put on their shabby prison garb, Corrie put her roll of clothing she had hidden under her dress. Seeing that it bulged so obviously, she asked the Lord to cause his angels to surround her so that the guards would not see her.

The women were checked carefully. Nothing escaped the glare of the prison matrons' eyes. The woman just in front of Corrie had hidden a woolen vest which was found and taken from her. But they let Corrie pass by as though they did not even see her while Betsie, who was just behind her, was thoroughly searched.

But then they had to pass through another line and another search. Eyes that missed nothing looked the prisoners over, and each woman was felt so that nothing would be overlooked. But, again, Corrie passed by unseen and untouched.

Bolstered by the angelic intervention, Corrie prayed with joy in her heart: "O Lord, if thou dost so answer prayer, I can face even Ravensbruck unafraid."

Attitude

You probably don't recognize the name of Alice James, but she was the sister of William and Henry James. Henry James was a distinguished American writer. William James, the father of American pragmatic philosophy, was also well known.

Sister Alice was never as well known as her two brothers, but she was a sensitive and caring person.

An invalid from the age of eighteen until she died at forty, Alice James possessed a radiant spirit. Reading through her journal, one would never guess she was an invalid.

While reading George Eliot's letters in which Eliot (pseudonym of Mary Ann Evans) frequently complained of her aches and pains, Alice once asked, "Where was the creature's pride?"

And her biographer writes about Alice: "She never accepted the horizons of invalidism."

Alice James had a problem, to be sure. But she didn't compound her physical problems with the added problem of a poor attitude.

The lesson she has taught us ought to be remembered.

Beauty

Beauty may be only skin deep, but moderns spend a lot of money trying to improve the looks of that millimeter of epidermis. It is massaged, manicured, pedicured, paraffined, steamed, injected, lifted, packed with seaweed, mud, milk, and night cream. And sometimes it helps.

When archeologists unearthed a 5,000-year-old makeup kit in a royal tomb in Babylonia, they said it was the earliest dependable evidence of the use of cosmetics. But some diehards still believe the practice started with Eve.

At least one thing is certain: moderns didn't invent beauty potions. Galen, a second-century physician, perfected a beauty cream which consisted of oil, beeswax, and water. Although cosmetics of the early Christian era were crude and sometimes dangerous, they were used. Even way back then the skin was cleansed with creams. Then lubricants, powder, rouge, moisturizers, wrinkle cream, brow color, suntan lotion, dandruff remover, and hair dye were used.

And the quest for beauty is an endless one. One survey taken not many years ago revealed that 1,200 new beauty products were put on the market in a five-year span. But 1,000 of them were soon dropped by manufacturers.

Few of us would discourage either the macho man or the delicate lady from trying to improve on nature. But real beauty comes from within. And the most exotic beauty treatment ever concocted cannot cover up the ugly lines that sin draws on the countenance.

The psalmist wrote about the beauty that cannot fade and that ought to be diligently sought when he wrote in Psalm 90:17: "Let the beauty of the Lord our God be upon us."

Believe

Scottish minister Ian MacPherson told about walking down a street in Wales one cold winter day, watching a man who was struggling against the cold north wind.

MacPherson said that when the man came to a certain place in the road, he reached in his pocket for the key to his home. Walking up to the front door of the house, the man inserted the key in the lock and walked out of the cold into the warmth of his own home.

"It was the name of the house that fascinated me," MacPherson said. For written above the front door was the Latin word *Credo*—"I believe."

What you have written upon your heart will determine the direction you take. According to Jesus, *believe* is the golden key that unlocks all of heaven's treasures to us.[†]

Bible

While Benjamin Franklin was living in Paris, he joined a literary society. Made up of men who claimed to be infidels, the men would meet, read papers they had prepared, and criticize them.

The day came when it was Franklin's turn to present a paper. Copying the Book of Ruth, he read the Old Testament love story without revealing its identity. When he had finished, the chairman requested Mr. Franklin to let them publish his paper.

"I am sorry, Sir, but the story has already been printed. You will find it in the Bible which you claim to despise," Franklin replied.

The Bible is not only the most popular book that has ever been printed; it is also the most neglected and most misunderstood. Yet it contains all the wisdom of the ages.[†]

Blood

Martin Luther lived during the sixteenth century. An Augustinian monk, Luther was a catalyst for the Protestant Reformation.

In spite of his greatness and his monumental contribution to history, Luther was easily given to melancholy and depression.

In one of his periods of depression, Luther said he seemed to see a hideous form listing his sins on the wall of his room.

The list was long and terrible. Luther saw his sinful words, sinful deeds, open sins and secret sins—sins of omission and commission. Luther said there seemed to be no end to the list.

Powerless to stop the hand that wrote on and on, Luther bowed his head and called upon the Savior. When he looked up, Luther said, the writer paused and gazed at him.

"You have forgotten something," Luther said.

"And what have I forgotten?" asked the demonic visitor.

"Take your pen and write one more thing," Luther commanded. "Write: 'The blood of Jesus Christ, his Son, cleanseth us from all sin.'"

At the mention of the blood of Jesus the demonic visitor disappeared, and the wall upon which it had been writing was perfectly clean.

Burdens

Do you carry a heavy load? Take heart, for multitudes have been there.

Lord Byron hobbled through life, dragging a club foot. Mrs. Robert Browning, one of the gentlest of writers, hardly ever enjoyed good health.

But what admirers of literature have not been moved by Byron? What lovers have not been thrilled by Browning's "Sonnets from the Portuguese"?

Burdens are a part of life, and the world is made better by courageous burden bearers.

After Scottish preacher Ian Maclaren died, it was said of him, "He had a great eye for the sunrise."

When the load is heavy, take heart. The sunrise is coming. The darkness will pass.[†]

Certainties

Lloyd Douglas, the author of *The Robe,* once told a story about a violin teacher who lived down the street from Douglas.

One morning when Douglas went to the studio, he asked his old friend, "And what's the good news for today?"

Holding up a tuning fork, the teacher struck the fork with a padded mallet and exclaimed, "The good news today is: that is *A.*

"The soprano down the hall misses her high notes, and the piano across the hall is off-key," the teacher replied. "But that, my friend, is *A.*

"It was *A* yesterday; it is *A* today; and it will be *A* tomorrow. The good news for today is: that is *A,* and it won't change."

There are some things that stabilize life in an unstable era. They are sure, unchanging, and dependable in an unsure, changing, and undependable world.

Paul had three of those certainties in mind when he wrote, "And now abideth faith, hope, charity, these three; but the greatest of these is charity" (1 Cor. 13:13).[†]

Character

Voltaire, the French philosopher and infidel, said, "When it is a question of money, everybody is of the same religion."

But that's not true. Baruch Spinoza, the seventeenth-century Dutch philosopher, made a humble living by grinding lenses. But as he worked, Spinoza thought great thoughts about God and man.

When King Louis XIV offered Spinoza a pension if the philosopher would dedicate only one of his books to the king, Spinoza refused to be bought.

Believing that personal character was more important than the king's patronage, Spinoza continued to live in poverty, polishing his lenses, and thinking his great thoughts about God and man.

So, contrary to Voltaire's thesis, everybody is not of the same religion when it comes to money.[†]

Christ

Bertel Thorvaldsen was one of Denmark's greatest sculptors. Born in 1770, Thorvaldsen died in 1844. Although Thorvaldsen did secular work, his best-loved works are the statues of Christ and the twelve apostles.

In a downtown cathedral in Copenhagen, Denmark, one can see the statues of Christ and the apostles by the famous sculptor. On the south wall are statues of six of the apostles, and on the north wall are the statues of the other six. Many who have seen Thorvaldsen's work say that he has caught the character of each apostle in the cold marble.

The statue of Christ is in the high altar of the church. The guides who take the visitors through the cathedral, I am told, say something like this to the visitors as they stand before the high altar: "For you fully to appreciate the face of Christ, you must kneel and look up."

There is a shaft of sunlight that comes through the roof and shines directly upon the face of Christ. Visitors who have knelt at the altar and have looked up into His face say that it is a moving experience to look at the face of Christ from a kneeling position.

Charles the Great, perhaps better known as Charlemagne, ruled the Franks from AD 768 to 814. From 800 to 814, he was "emperor of the Romans."

The first Germanic ruler to bear the title of emperor, Charlemagne's empire lasted for a thousand years after his death.

A strong military man who truly deserved the title of "the

Great," Charlemagne's longest military venture was the Saxon War. Rulers of all northeastern Germany, the Saxons were pagans and were defeated only after thirty years of war. But Charlemagne's victory led to the Christianization and civilization of Germany.

After his death in 814, Charlemagne was dressed as a true king for his burial. His robe was placed around him, the crown was placed on his head and his scepter was put in his hand. And on his lap lay the Gospels. He was then buried in an upright position beneath the chapel at Aachen, Germany.

When his tomb was opened in 1001 by Otto III, Charlemagne's body and burial apparatus were well preserved. The tomb was opened again in 1165 by Emperor Frederick I and reopened in 1215 by King Frederick II. Charlemagne's remains were removed at that time and put in casket made of silver and gold.

His remains were then installed in the cathedral inside a marble throne; for the next three centuries, the German emperors were crowned as they sat upon Charlemagne's throne.

But Jesus Christ was crucified on a Judean hillside, buried in the tomb of Joseph of Arimathea, and on the third day, He rose again.

Christ's throne is no earthly throne, and His kingdom is no earthly kingdom. In heaven, seated at the Father's right hand, He is the King of kings and the Lord of lords, and millions through the centuries have bowed reverently before him.

Julian, a Roman emperor who lived from AD 331 to 363, was called "the Apostate." He was the nephew of Constantine the Great, who christianized the Roman world. After Julian tried to restore pagan worship to the empire, he became known as "the

Apostate." He died from a wound which he received in a battle with the Persians.

Well-educated and liked by his troops, Julian marched into Persian territory in AD 362. His heart was set on conquering the ancient Persian Empire, and he would not be dissuaded.

Emperor Julian had a young aide who was a Christian. One day, Julian asked the young Christian, "What do you suppose your friend Jesus is doing today?"

"Sir," the young aide answered, "since Jesus is a carpenter, it may be that even today He is taking time off from building mansions for the faithful to build a coffin for you."

Before the day was over, Julian and his army had been surrounded by Persian soldiers; and in the bloody battle that followed, Julian was grievously wounded.

It is said that before his death, Julian gathered up a handful of dust from the battlefield, dust that was stained with his own blood, and flinging it toward the heavens cried, "Oh, Galilean, thou hast conquered!"

Many of the world's well-known personalities, both actual and mythical, have claimed a miraculous birth. The Greeks said Perseus was the son of Zeus (Jupiter), and that his mother was Danae, a virgin.

Jupiter, the king of gods in Roman mythology, was called Zeus by the ancient Greeks. His father was Saturn, and Jupiter was called an Olympian because it was believed he lived on Greece's Mount Olympus. He was the god of the heavens and the ruler of gods and men. According to mythology, Jupiter came down from heaven in a shower of gold.

According to a Hindu myth, Krishna was the son of a virgin Davaki. And the Greeks said that Alexander the Great, the son of Philip of Macedon and Olympias, was begotten by a serpent. His mother fired young Alexander's imagination by telling him that he was a descendant of Achilles and that his father, Philip, was a descendant of Hercules.

It was believed by the Romans that Caesar Augustus, the first of the Roman emperors and the one sitting upon Rome's throne when Jesus was born, was conceived by a serpent as Augustus's mother lay asleep in the temple of Apollo.

These fables believed by ancients failed to compare, however, with the birth of Jesus Christ. Conceived by the virgin Mary through the power of the Holy Spirit, Jesus Christ is the Son of God and the sinless Savior.

Comfort

Arthur John Gossip was born in Glasgow, Scotland, in 1873. He was a minister of the gospel who spent all of his life preaching in his native land. Dr. Gossip's wife died in 1927.

The first sermon he preached after his wife's dramatic and sudden death was titled "But When Life Tumbles In, What Then?"

It is a personal testimony in which Gossip talks about his great grief and the strength which his Friend and Savior gave to him.

There are some striking sentences in the sermon, but perhaps none is as striking as this one: "You people in the sunshine may believe the faith, but we in the shadow must believe it. We have nothing else."

In the next to the last paragraph of his masterful message, Gossip said: "I don't think you need to be afraid of life. Our hearts are very frail; and there are places where the road is very steep and very lonely. But we have a wonderful God."

Uncle Tom and two women—all slaves—sat huddled together around a campfire. The women were too exhausted from the day's work to grind their corn for the evening meal, so Tom did it for them. Returning his kindness, the women baked Tom's cakes for him.

One of the women, upon seeing Tom pull out his Bible, asked, "What's dat book?"

"Why, woman, dat's de Bible," Tom answered.

"Lawsa mercy," she replied, "what's dat? Read a piece of it," she said.

"Come unto me, all ye that labour and are heavy laden, and I will give you rest," Tom read.

"My, my," she sighed, "dem's good words! Who says dem?"

"Why, woman," Tom explained, "dem's Jesus' words."

They are good words, these words of Jesus. And millions of suffering saints have found comfort in them.†

Commitment

In London's Westminster Abbey, one of the first graves one will see upon entering the majestic cathedral is that of missionary David Livingstone. On Livingstone's marker in the floor are written the words of Jesus: "And other sheep I have, which are not of this fold: them also I must bring . . ." (John 10:16).

Sent out by the Church of Scotland to Africa as a missionary-physician, Dr. Livingstone served there for more than three decades.

A South African mission society wrote Livingstone that they had some good men they would like to send to help him. And they inquired if there were a good road leading to where Livingstone was currently serving.

Livingstone wrote back to the society: "If you have men who will come only if they know there is a good road, I don't want them. I want men who will come if there is no road."[†]

Compassion

Dr. Albert Schweitzer began his work as a medical missionary at Lambarene, French Equatorial Africa, in 1913. As the years passed, Schweitzer built a large hospital and medical station there. And in that hospital, thousands of Africans were treated yearly.

In 1952, he won the Nobel Peace Prize for his work in Africa. But, rather than spending the $33,000 prize money on himself, he used the money to expand his hospital and to set up a leper colony.

When Schweitzer first went to Africa, he was treating a man in his small hospital. Weak and desperately ill, the man still had hope that the Christian missionary would be able to help him.

Looking up into the haggard face of the doctor, the man asked, "Who sent you here?"

And the kind, compassionate physician answered, "The man of Nazareth sent me."[†]

Confusion

In 1930, Marc Connelly won a Pulitzer Prize for his play titled *Green Pastures*. The play dramatizes early American Negro religious beliefs.

In the play, the angel Gabriel is sent down from heaven to investigate the havoc that Noah's flood has created.

Returning to heaven to make his report to God, Gabriel says: "Lord, there ain't nothin' fastened down there, anymore. Everythin' nailed down is comin' loose."

That seems to be the kind of world in which we are living today. Everything that is nailed down seems to be coming loose.

Conversion

F. B. Meyer was an English Baptist minister. Born in London on April 8, 1847, Meyer was reared in a devout Baptist home. In his preaching ministry which spanned more than sixty years, Meyer preached more than sixteen thousand sermons. But Meyer, who died in 1929, called himself "Just God's errand boy."

In one of his sermons, Meyer tells about an ugly tugboat that ran between London and Portsmouth. She was terribly battered from the careless way in which she had been handled. She was so scarred from the many collisions that she had been nicknamed "Old Bust Me Up."

Watching "Old Bust Me Up" come into the dock was always a humorous sight for the sailors and crewman on shore. She never glided like a swan into dock; rather, she collided with the other vessels, rammed into the sides of the docks, and was just generally clumsy.

One day, however, to the amazement of all who stood on dock watching her come in, "Old Bust Me Up" slid into the dock as straight as an arrow. She glided like a graceful swan into her berth without touching any of the other docked vessels. One old seaman was so amazed at the way she was being handled that he called out to the old, battered boat: "Ho, there, 'Old Bust Me Up,' what's the matter with you?"

And back from the old vessel came the reply: "I'm the same old boat, but I have a new skipper on board."

That's the difference. When one receives Jesus Christ as his or her personal Savior, everything changes. The "New Skipper on board" is what makes the difference.

Capt. Edward V. Rickenbacker was America's greatest air ace in World War I. He is credited with having shot down four balloons and twenty-two enemy airplanes.

In 1942, about a year after World War II broke out, Rickenbacker was asked by Secretary of War Henry Stimson to make an inspection trip for him. On that trip out over the Pacific Ocean, Rickenbacker's plane had mechanical trouble; and he and the crew of seven men were force down in the Pacific, six hundred miles north of the Island of Samoa. For twenty-four days, they drifted in rubber rafts on the Pacific, and the world despaired for their lives.

After Capt. Rickenbacker was rescued, he returned to the United States. One day he was invited to address a large group of disabled veterans in a rehabilitation hospital.

In what he said to the disabled veterans that day, one sentence stands out above all the others: "Men, if you have not had an experience of God in your life, my advice is to get busy and get yourself one."

That's the thing people need most. We Christians call it conversion.

Cross

After Napoleon and his troops had run roughshod over Europe, they paused to rejoice in their victory. Calling his generals together, Napoleon showed them a map of the world. Pointing to England, which was represented by a red dot on the map, Napoleon said to his generals, "If it were not for that dot, we could conquer the world."

Napoleon spoke prophetically, for that red dot became the English Duke of Wellington and Waterloo, Belgium, where Wellington defeated Napoleon and his army.

The cross is God's holy, red dot in history. And Satan knows that were it not for that red dot on Golgatha, he could conquer all. But because of the cross, Satan's doom is sealed.

Thousands have died upon crosses. A cross kind of death was not uncommon in the ancient world. Darius crucified three thousand captives at the seige of Babylon. Alexander the Great crucified two thousand when his vengeance fell on Tyre. One historian writes that the crosses on Tyre's bloody shores were more numerous than the masts of ships in her harbor.

Many men have hung upon crosses. It was not an uncommon thing in the first century to see some blood-drenched corpse hanging upon a cross, blackening in the hot sun. When Titus took Jerusalem, it is said that there wasn't enough wood to build the crosses Titus needed for the condemned Jews.

In her *Life of Lacordaire,* author Dora Greenwell described the fanatical austerities to which Lacordaire subjected himself one Good Friday.

Descending the stairs into the crypt of a famous Paris church,

Lacordaire walked in the semidarkness among the vaults filled with bones until he found some wood. Then building a crude cross, Lacordaire bound himself upon the cross, staying there for three hours.

But the thousands of crosses erected on a score of bloody hillsides in history, and the cross of Lacordaire, all have this in common: They have no saving efficacy.

But the cross of Jesus does. Although there were three crosses on Calvary the day the Lord was slain, only the sacrifice of the middle cross saves from sin.

An artist once painted a picture of a solitary man, rowing his small boat across a stormy lake. It was midnight, and the churning waves beat against the tiny craft, determined to destroy it.

But in his scene of what looked like a midnight tragedy, the artist painted a lone star shining in the midnight blackness. The oarsman had his eye upon the star as he labored against the angry waves.

Beneath the pictures, the artist inscribed the words: "If I lose sight of that, I am lost."

The cross is our North Star. If we lose sight of that, we are eternally lost. It is only by the preaching of the cross that we can be saved.

Sir John Bowring was a Britisher who was knighted in 1854 because of his faithful service to the Crown. He served as Britain's representative to France, counsul to Hong Kong, and later governor of Hong Kong. Bowring also served in the British Parliament on two occasions and was the master of thirteen different languages.

Once Bowring was taken to see Saint Paul's Cathedral which was built in the seventeenth century. However, when Bowring was there, all that was standing of the magnificent cathedral was the front facade and the cross, high atop the ruins of the church.

Bowring was so impressed by the cross towering over the ruins of Saint Paul's that he wrote the magnificent Christian hymn: "In the Cross of Christ I Glory."

One can almost see Saint Paul's cross in Bowring's hymn:

> In the cross of Christ I glory,
> Tow'ring o'er the wrecks of time
> All the light of sacred story
> Gathers round its head sublime.

All of our hope rests in the cross of Christ. Knowing this, the apostle Paul refused to glory "save in the cross of Christ."

When Dr. Theodore Adams, pastor of First Baptist Church, Richmond, Virginia, was president of the Baptist World Alliance, he visited some Baptist missionary stations in the Philippines.

It was shortly after the close of World War II, and missionary Ted Badger took Dr. Adams to a prison compound where some American missionaries had been imprisoned by the Japanese.

Missionary Badger explained to Dr. Adams that one day American bombers passed overhead in the shape of the cross, conveying the message to the missionaries that no destructive bombs would be dropped on them. They knew they were safe because of the cross.

Death

Dr. Gaston Foote, noted Methodist minister who served First Methodist Church, Fort Worth, Texas, told about one of his visits to Scotland. While Foote was there, he was told about a member of the church in that community who had recently died. He was the last surviving member of his family.

When the old man became too weak to attend the services of his church, his pastor regularly visited him. The pastor related that by the side of the old man's bed was an empty chair the old man had reserved for Jesus. All who visited with him knew not to sit in that chair. It was a special chair, reserved for his special Friend.

One morning, a neighbor of the old man called the pastor. "Pastor," he said, "our friend is very sick, and you need to come as soon as possible."

When the pastor arrived at the humble home, the old man had already slipped away into the land beyond. He was half sitting up in bed, and his right arm was around the back of the chair which he had reserved for Jesus.

How comforting it must have been to the old gentleman, when it came time for him to cross over the river into heaven, to put his arm around the shoulder of his Elder Brother and walk with Him to the Father's house.

But each of us who is a believer will have that same privilege. We won't go that way alone.

In May 1915, a German submarine sank the *Lusitania*, an American passenger vessel, off the coast of Ireland. There were

1,924 people on board the *Lusitania*. Of that number, 1,198 of them lost their lives. And the sinking of the *Lusitania* contributed to American's entry into World War I.

A torpedo quickly cut its way through the waters and exploded into the ship with a sickening roar. When the people realized what had happened, they panicked and rushed for the lifeboats.

But Charles Frohman, one of the 128 Americans on board, didn't move. As he stood peacefully by the rail of the listing ship, a passenger rushed by on his way to the lifeboat and asked, "Aren't you afraid?"

"Afraid? No," Frohman answered. "Why fear death? It is the most beautiful adventure of life."

It can be—and it is—for those who know Jesus Christ as their personal Savior.

Once an Oriental sultan gave his scribe the monumental task of writing the history of the human race. The scribe worked faithfully at his almost-impossible task for many years. When he had finished, he loaded his five hundred volumes of history on the backs of one hundred donkeys and brought them to his master.

The sultan looked at the mountain of material and commanded his scribe to shorten it.

"Abridge it!" the sultan angrily shouted. "It's too long to be read!"

"Very well, sire" the scribe humbly responded. "These five hundred volumes can be abbreviated into one sentence: 'They were born; they suffered; they died!'"

Such is the lot, as Job says, of man that is born of a woman.

"Wherefore, as by one man sin entered into the world, and death by sin; and so death passed upon all men, for that all have sinned." (Rom. 5:12).

Auguste Rodin, the greatest French sculptor in the second half of the nineteenth century, graphically portrayed the truthfulness of Paul's statement.

Rodin carved three figures: Adam, Eve, and their son, Abel. Abel is dead, slain by Cain, his brother.

The couple is walking. They are on their way to bury Abel. Adam is holding the limp body of his precious son in his arms.

Eve is looking up at Adam. There are tears in her eyes and an unknowing look on her face. Adam's features are strong and commanding, but his heart is broken as he looks down upon the limp form he is carrying.

Rodin called it *The First Funeral*.

But it wasn't the last. And until Jesus comes in glory, men and women, boys and girls, will continue to die.

Dedication

During the tragic War between the States, Gen. Robert E. Lee once sent word to Gen. Stonewall Jackson that if he happened to be in the area, Lee would like to see him.

When Jackson received Lee's request, a terrible storm was breaking across his lines. Despite the storm, Jackson mounted his horse and rode all night in response to his commander's request.

Jackson finally reached Lee's camp tired and soaked to the bone. Lee was surprised and asked, "Why did you ride through such a terrible storm?"

Jackson's reply was simple: "Sir, the least request from my general is a command to me."

Defeat

Thomas Carlyle once said, "God sits in heaven and does nothing."

If we were honest, probably each of us would confess that we have felt like that at times. Life often closes in on us, and we pray, but no answer comes. We each wonder, at times like that, where God is.

A disheartened Englishman, all but washed out by life, confessed that he didn't know what he believed, but, "I don't believe all this 'God is love' stuff," he said.

Then, reviewing his life, he said he had been in two world wars, hadn't been able to find a job for eighteen months, and had seen his wife die from cancer.

"Now," he said, "I am waiting for the atomic bomb to fall."

Then, in a final expression of desperation and defeat, he bitterly said, "All that stuff about Jesus is no help."

But we need to remember that it is in just such an hour of defeat when the darkness surrounds us, that we very well may find God.

A friend who had been in the M. D. Anderson Hospital in Houston, being treated surgically for a malignant growth behind one of her eyeballs, confessed to me, "God had to strike me blind before I could see."

Dependability

David Livingstone was a missionary to Africa for more than three decades. Born in Blantyre, Scotland, March 19, 1813, he died in Central Africa in 1874. At his request, Livingstone's heart was cut from his bosom and buried in Africa. His body was then carried nine hundred miles overland and put on a ship bound for London. Livingstone was buried in Westminster Abbey.

After having received his medical degree from Glasgow University in 1840, Livingstone went to South Africa as a missionary under the auspices of the London Missionary Society. He not only wanted to convert the natives to Christianity, but he also wanted to put an end to the terrible slave trade and discover the source of the Nile River.

Once during his missionary service in Africa, Livingstone was surrounded by a group of angry natives. It looked like the end had come for the valiant missionary.

Going into his tent, Livingstone got down on his knees and opened his Bible to the promise of Jesus who had commissioned him to go to Africa: "Lo, I am with you alway, even unto the end of the world" (Matt. 28:20).

Arising from his knees, Dr. Livingstone noted in his diary: "That's the word of a gentleman. He will keep His word to me." And with that, he undressed and went to bed and had a good night's sleep.

When Livingstone returned to Africa from England in 1866, he set out on a long, torturous journey to find the source of the Nile River. When months went by and the world did not hear anything from him, a New York newspaper sent Sir Henry Morton Stanley on an expedition to find Livingstone. Almost everybody knows the story of their meeting as the names Stanley and Livingstone became linked in history.

Refusing to return to civilization with Stanley in 1872, Livingstone continued his labors and traveled for another year.

But age and the physical hardships he had suffered for years caught up with him at Lake Bangweulu where he died on April 30, 1873.

During his more than three decades in Africa, Livingstone discovered that God is trustworthy and dependable. This is a personal discovery which each of us must make. But having discovered it, life can never again be the same for us.

The divine dependability is both a spiritual and physical fact.

For example, the earth rotates on its axis at about 1,100 miles an hour. If it rotated at only one hundred miles an hour, our days and nights would be ten times as long as they are. The nights would be so long and cold that nearly all growing things would freeze. And the days would be so long and hot that what survives would be scorched.

The surface temperature of the sun is about 11,000°F. Its average distance from the earth is 92.9 million miles. It is just far enough away from us to warm us. If it were nearer, causing the temperature on earth to change as much as 50 degrees in a single year, human beings and all vegetation would roast.

The earth is tilted on its axis at an angle of 23 degrees. This gives us our four seasons. If it were not tilted, the North and South Poles would be in eternal twilight. The water from the oceans would move north and south and pile up huge continents of ice, leaving only a briny desert between the equator and the ice. The lurching of the ocean would diminish the rainfall in parts of the world, and the outcome would be catastrophic.

The moon, 240,000 miles away from the earth, reminds us twice daily of its presence by causing the tides to rise and fall. Twice each day, the crust of the earth is bent outward several inches by the pull of the moon. But it is done so gently that we hardly notice that the level of the oceans are lifted several feet toward the moon when the earth's crust is bent.

But if our moon were only 50,000 miles away, its pull would be so strong that the tides would be enormous. Twice daily, the tides would inundate all lowlands of the continents of the world and erode the mountains as well. Under the mighty pull of the moon, the crust of the earth would break, and ensuing hurricanes, created by huge tidal waves, would destroy multitudes of people daily.

But the universe is dependable because Almighty God, who created it, is dependable.

Despair

Voltaire, the noted French philosopher of the eighteenth century, once said: "I wish I had never been born."

Lord Byron, one of England's most famous poets, confessed on his deathbed at thirty-six:

> My days are in the yellow leaf;
> The flowers and fruits of love are gone;
> The worm, the canker, the grief
> Are mine alone!

Jay Gould, a famous American railroad philanthropist of the last century, said when dying: "I suppose I am the most miserable man ever to live."

And Benjamin Disraeli, also known as Lord Beaconsfield, onetime prime minister of Great Britain, wrote about life: "Youth is a mistake, manhood a struggle, old age a regret."

Determination

An old gypsy woman in Warsaw saw little Marja Sklodowska playing one day and demanded to see her hand. Looking at her palm, the gypsy told Marja that someday she would be famous.

Marja grew up to become Madame Curie who, along with her husband Pierre, discovered radium.

As a young woman Marja wanted to become a scientist, but she was denied admittance to the University of Cracow. Determined, she went to Paris and was accepted by the Sorbonne.

The quest for radium took the best years of her life. She refused to quit even when her health broke.

But Marie and husband Pierre's determination paid off. They gave to the world the miracle of radium.[†]

Told he was losing his hearing, the most devastating physical problem that could face a musician, Beethoven responded, "I will take life by the throat."

When noted Scottish romantic novelist Sir Walter Scott was bankrupted by his publishers, Scott declared, "No man will say poor fellow to me; my own right hand will pay the debt."

And when Salvation Army founder William Booth was told blindness was approaching, the old soldier of the cross responded: "I have used my sight for Jesus; now I will use my blindness for Him."

As a young man, Winston Churchill attended Harrow preparatory school. But he showed little academic skill, graduating in the lower part of his class.

Many years after his graduation from Harrow, when he was prime minister, Churchill was invited to return to Harrow to speak to the student body.

Attempting to prepare the students for the prime minister's visit, the headmaster told them to listen carefully because Churchill was one of England's most eloquent orators.

When the morning came for Churchill to speak, he acknowledged the introduction given to him by the headmaster.

Looking sternly at the young student body, he scowled: "Young gentlemen, never give up! Never give up! Never give up! Never! Never! Never! Never! Never!"

And he sat down. But it was a speech the students would never forget.[†]

Difficulties

Each of us lives with difficulties of some kind. But we can succeed in spite of them.

English poet Thomas Gray once wrote that "low spirits are my true and faithful companions." But when one reads his "Elegy in a Country Churchyard," which he wrote seventy-five times before he had it as he wanted it, one understands why it is one of the best-known poems in the English language.

Cervantes started *Don Quixote* while he was a prisoner in jail. John Bunyan wrote *The Pilgrim's Progress* during the twelve years he was in Bedford jail. And Victor Hugo, France's most popular literary figure, wrote *Les Miserables* which was published simultaneously in ten languages while he was in Napoleon III's jail.

If we succeed in life, most of us will have to do it in spite of some things.[†]

Discouragement

Discouragement tries the best and the worst of us. It is no respecter of persons.

Henry Ward Beecher, one of America's finest early-day preachers, became so discouraged at one point in his ministry that he was ready to quit.

Pastor of a small church in Indianapolis, Beecher made up his mind to give up the ministry. He said he had only about twenty church members: nineteen of them were women, and the other one was a "no-account man."

Beecher confessed he had preached in the Indianapolis church for three years without making a sinner wink!

Born in Connecticut in 1813, Beecher had a speech impediment that he had to work hard to overcome. He overcame both his speech impediment and his desire to quit the ministry because of discouragement. Beecher's efforts made him an eloquent Presbyterian and Congregationalist preacher whose ability earned him a prominent place among American clergymen.[†]

Easter

Arturo Toscanini may have been the greatest musical conductor of modern times. Born in Parma, Italy, on March 15, 1867, Toscanini died in New York City in 1957.

Toscanini became the principal conductor of La Scalla in Milan, Italy, in 1898. He came to the United States in 1908 and conducted at the Metropolitan Opera in New York City until 1950. From 1937 to 1953, he directed the National Broadcasting Symphony Orchestra.

Though Toscanini was a great man, he had a terrible fear of death. Each time he saw a floral wreath, it reminded him of death. But his admirers did not know of his fear. One evening one of them laid a wreath at the maestro's feet after a presentation by the orchestra. When Toscanini saw the wreath, he turned pale, stood paralyzed for a moment, then rushed out a side door. With the speed of a young athlete, the white-haired maestro ran through the crowds on Seventh Avenue.

When Bruno Zirato, the Philharmonic manager, saw Toscanini rush out the side door, he knew what was wrong. But as he ran after the conductor Zirato fell far behind, for he was no match for Toscanini.

Fleeing at top speed down the crowded avenue and into Times Square, Toscanini rushed into his hotel, bounded up the stairs to his room, and locked himself in for the night.

The fear of death is man's greatest fear. But Jesus conquered our worst fear. On the first Easter Sunday morning, He stood outside the open tomb and addressed that fear with the words that would be heard around the world: "I am alive for evermore."[†]

As a child, Marja Sklodowska decided to become a scientist. One day in her native Warsaw, an old gypsy woman stopped Marja and asked to see her palm. Looking at the lines in the little girl's hand, the gypsy told Marja she would be very famous someday.

You know the little girl as Madame Curie. Along with her husband Pierre, Madame Curie discovered radium. There is absolutely no way to estimate the importance of their discovery.

One day her beloved Pierre was struck by an automobile and killed on the streets of Paris. They had been very close. In fact, their lives had been so entwined that one almost breathed for the other.

On the night after Pierre's funeral, his widow went home and wrote in her diary:

> They filled the grave and put sheaves of flowers on it. Everything is over. Pierre is sleeping his last sleep beneath the earth. It is the end of everything, everything, everything.

That was how the disciples of Jesus felt on Good Friday when He was nailed to the cross. All of their hopes and ambitions died on Golgotha with Jesus.

But Sunday morning changed everything. Before the day was over, all of the disciples, except Thomas, had seen and talked to the resurrected Lord. As suddenly as He had been taken from them, Jesus was back in their midst.

And as suddenly as sorrow had fallen upon them, joy overwhelmed them.

June 18, 1815, was a significant day in history. On that day the British army commanded by "the Iron Duke," the Duke of Wellington, defeated the French army commanded by Napoleon "the Little Colonel." Wellington's victory put an end to Napoleon's bloody career at Waterloo, Belgium.

The good news of Napoleon's defeat, sent by signals, was relayed to Winchester Cathedral. Those in the cathedral that day strained their eyes and slowly began to read: "W-e-l-l-i-n-g-t-o-n d-e-f-e-a-t-e-d . . ."

But as the message was being read at Winchester, the fog rolled in, and the signals were no longer visible.

"Wellington has been defeated!" the people cried. The sad news spread quickly, bringing despair and hopelessness to all who heard it.

But the message they read was incomplete. When the fog lifted, watchers on Winchester Cathedral got the whole story, for the signal read: "W-e-l-l-i-n-g-t-o-n d-e-f-e-a-t-e-d t-h-e e-n-e-m-y!"

When the people got the whole story, everything changed. The gloom that had settled over the countryside gave way to gladness when the people discovered that Wellington had stopped Napoleon.

On the Friday that Jesus was crucified, the disciples' world was swathed in darkness. "It is all over," they sighed to each other as they huddled behind their closed doors. "What shall we do, and where shall we turn?" they sadly asked.

But they didn't have all the story. On Easter Sunday morning, Jesus was raised from the dead, and everything suddenly changed for the disciples. Friday's gloom gave way to Sunday's gladness when the disciples learned that Jesus was alive.

Faith

The plant Uranus was discovered in 1781. It was thought to be the outermost planet from the earth.

But as astronomers studied Uranus, they noticed that it behaved strangely. They wondered if the strange behavior of the planet could be caused by a neighboring planet which had not yet been discovered.

They studied their charts and came to the conclusion that an undiscovered planet was affecting Uranus's behavior. Then carefully training their telescopes on that place in the heavens where they calculated the new planet had to be, they waited patiently.

For sixty-five years they waited and watched, and their suspicions were confirmed on September 14, 1886.

Shortly after midnight on that epochal night, an astronomer focused his telescope on the distant spot and suddenly spotted Neptune, a planet that had never before been seen.

How was it discovered? Training, careful study, and hard work played a significant role. The astronomers had weighed the evidence, made their mathematical calculations, and came to the conclusion that there was another planet nearby.

But faith discovered it. Faith had told them, "It's out there! Don't give up. It's there!"

Reason gives its evidence for the presence of God in the world, but it is faith that discovers Him.

Adolf Hitler and his Nazi madmen exterminated twelve million people during World War II. Some were executed by firing squads, and others died in gas chambers. Seven million of those killed by the Nazis were Christians, and another five million were Jews.

One of those hideous death camps was at Auschwitz. There, seven thousand Germans worked to carry out the satanic schemes of the mustached paperhanger. Seventeen tons of gold were pulled from the mouths of Hitler's victims at Auschwitz, their bodies were consumed in the gas chambers, and their ashes were used to fertilize German victory gardens.

Fatty acids from their bodies were salvaged to make inexpensive soap. A Danzig soap manufacturing firm revealed the formula that they used: twelve pounds of human fat, ten quarts of water, and eight ounces to a pound of caustic soda. Boil for two to three hours, then cool.

What was it that gave those Jews and Christians courage to face their terrible ordeal?

Why, the answer is simple: it was their faith in God. Faith nerved them. Faith gave them the courage to accept what they could not change.

When Christopher Columbus left Spain on August 3, 1492, for his voyage to the West, few believed in him or his cause. "You will fall off the edge of the earth," they said. "There is nothing beyond the Pillars of Hercules."

But Columbus wouldn't be stopped. "There is more beyond," he said to his critics. "And I will prove it to you."

Weeks out from port, the discouraged crew spotted evidence that land was near as leaves, branches, and wood floated by.

At 2:00 AM on October 12, they spotted the white sands of the Bahamas and took possession of a new world.

Faith stands at the lookout. Shielding its eyes against the blinding glare of a doubting world, it sees and embraces the eternal One.

And that brings hope to the heaviest heart on the darkest night.[†]

Faithfulness

A faithful old pastor was told by his superior that something was wrong with his work. "Only one person has been added to your church this year, and he is only a boy," the superior said.

Later that day, heavy of heart, the pastor was praying when someone walked up behind him. Turning around, he saw the boy—his only convert that year.

"Pastor, do you think I could become a preacher or a missionary?" he asked.

The lad was Robert Moffat who was destined to open Africa to the gospel of Jesus.

Years later when Moffat spoke in London, a young doctor heard him say: "I have seen in the morning sun the smoke of a thousand villages where no missionary has ever been."

The young doctor, deeply moved by Moffat's message, was David Livingstone. In 1840, he sailed for Africa where he labored for Jesus for more than three decades.[†]

Fear

One of England's greatest preachers was Alexander Maclaren. When he was sixteen years old, Maclaren relates, he went to work at Glasgow, six miles from his home. He would walk to Glasgow on Monday morning and return home after work on Saturday night.

Between his home and Glasgow, however, there was a deep ravine that was supposed to be haunted. It had a bad name because some crimes had been committed in the ravine. Because of the ravine's reputation, young Alexander was afraid to walk through it even during the daytime. To go through it at night was almost out of the question.

But one Monday morning as Maclaren was getting ready to walk to Glasgow to work, his father came to him and said: "Alec, come home as fast as you can Saturday night when you get off from work."

Young Maclaren thought of that deep, scary ravine and quickly answered his father: "Father, I will be awfully tired Saturday night. Why don't I wait and come home early Sunday morning?"

But his father wouldn't yield. He told him that since he would be gone five days, he needed to come on home Saturday night after work. And Alexander, reluctantly, agreed to do as his father requested.

All during that week, Alexander worried about that dark, frightening ravine that he would have to cross on Saturday night. By the time Saturday night came, he was more frightened than ever. But wrapping up his few belongings in a bundle, he started out on the dark road toward home.

Maclaren said that as he approached the ravine, he whistled loudly to keep up his courage. But when he got there and looked down into that terrible gulch, he felt he just couldn't go through it.

As he stood there shaking with fear, he suddenly heard footsteps coming up behind him. Looking around, he saw the head and shoulders of a man silhouetted against the pale moonlight. Just as he started to break and run, he recognized his father.

Mr. Maclaren knew that the boy would be scared to death, so he had come out to meet him. But being the wise father that he was, he said nothing to Alexander about the boy's fear, he told the boy instead, that he just wanted to see him so badly that he decided to meet him at the ravine. Shoulder to shoulder, they walked through the valley and on home together. All the fear that had been in the boy's heart was dispelled by the presence of his father.

When the way is the hardest and life is the most frightening, the presence of Jesus with us comforts and sustains us.

Clara Barton, the founder of the American Red Cross, was called "the Angel of the Battlefield" during the Civil War.

Born on a farm outside Oxford, Massachusetts, on Christmas Day 1821, Clara was terribly timid as a child. In the presence of others, even her own family, Clara was very quiet and shy. Fear so paralyzed her that she could hardly speak to her mother about her most personal needs.

Perhaps young Clara's first opportunity really to do something meaningful for someone else came when her brother David became seriously ill. For a period of three years, Clara was his nurse and companion.

She began to teach school when she was only sixteen. But in the country school classroom, some days Clara would be so scared that she couldn't look her pupils in the eye. Some days she would read to her students at great lengths because she was afraid to look at them. But out on the school grounds when Clara would see a frightened boy being bullied by another boy, she would become fearless, defending the underdog like a lioness defending her cubs.

Clara soon discovered that she could overcome her timidity by helping others. So, shortly after the outbreak of the Civil War in 1861, forty-year-old Clara Barton began to carry supplies to the wounded men on the battlefields, nursing them in their times of need. Although the United States government refused to help or encourage her, she managed to get a pass that admitted her to some of the worst battles of the war. Often under fire for hours, Clara Barton became known as "the Angel of the Battlefield."

At the conclusion of the war, Clara became involved in searching for missing soldiers. Forming and heading up a bureau for that very purpose, she and her bureau marked more than twelve thousand graves in the Andersonville, Georgia, National Cemetery.

When the war was ended, Clara Barton needed a cause. She went to Switzerland in 1869 during the Franco-Persian War and served as a battlefront nurse. There she had the opportunity to see the good work being done by the International Red Cross. Thus, when she returned home in 1873, she began to talk to people about the work of the Red Cross. When the American Red Cross was founded, Clara Barton was its first president.

Barton was active in such causes as the yellow-fever epidemics in Florida in 1877; the Johnstown, Pennsylvania, flood of 1889; and the relief in the Galveston, Texas, hurricane in 1900.

In spite of her fear, Clara Barton refused to quit and give up. Like so many before and after her, she discovered that courage is not the absence of fear, but it is going on when one is afraid to do so.

Fool

One of England's greatest statesmen was William E. Gladstone. An outstanding lay leader in the Church of England, he served as prime minister of Great Britain from 1868 through 1874.

A young man once visited Mr. Gladstone and told him that he would like to study law.

"Yes," Gladstone replied, "and what then?"

"Then I hope to be admitted to the Bar of England," he replied.

"Yes," Gladstone said, "and what then?"

"Then I would like to serve in Parliament, in the House of Lords," the young man replied.

"Yes," Gladstone answered, "and what then?"

"Then I hope I will be able to retire and happily live out the rest of my days."

"Yes," Gladstone said, "and what then?"

"Well," the young man replied, "then I suppose I will die."

"Yes," Gladstone soberly answered, "and what then?"

"I have no plans beyond that," the young man replied. "I have never thought any further than that."

"Then," Gladstone sternly replied, "young man, you are a fool. You need to go home and think life through."

Forgiveness

Seventy-five ancient pyramids of the Pharaohs still stand in the desert of Egypt. The ancient Egyptians believed there was life after death, and the pharaohs built the pyramids as tombs where their bodies could be preserved. In these vast tombs were placed objects which the pharaoh would need in the life to come.

The most magnificent of the pyramids is the Great Pyramid. Completed by Pharaoh Khufu in 2600 BC, the pyramid contains 2,300,000 stone blocks, each averaging two and one-half tons. Standing 451 feet tall, the weight of the pyramid is about 6.8 million tons. Forty men were needed to move each stone into place, and at least 100,000 slaves worked twenty years before the Great Pyramid was completed.

Standing forty stories tall, the base of the pyramid is so large that eight football fields could be placed beneath it. Yet in the building of this magnificent structure, it was measured so accurately, using only a knotted string, that it is only off one half of an inch along one 750-foot side. No wonder it is one of the Seven Wonders of the ancient world.

But there is something more magnificent and marvelous than even this wonder of the ancient world. It is the grace of God that brings forgiveness to a ruined and marred sinner, sets his or her feet upon the Solid Rock, and puts a song in the heart.

Future

John Hunt was a mountain climber. Before he began his dangerous climb of Mount Everest, the world's highest mountain, a friend asked him what he thought it would be like at the top.

Hunt replied that he didn't know. Then, as he approached the summit, Hunt replied: "It is usually obscured by clouds and squalls, and the road ahead is cloaked in mystery and uncertainty."

Although the future is cloaked in uncertainty, and we do not know what it holds, we know who holds the future, and we can trust it to Him whose eyelids never close in sleep and whose arms never grow weary.

Grace

Nicolaus Copernicus was born at Thorn, Poland, in 1473. He died in 1543.

An astronomer and scientist, Copernicus was the founder of modern astronomy. Fourteen hundred years before Copernicus's times, Ptolemy had written that the earth is the center of the universe and that it has no motion.

But Copernicus disputed Ptolemy's theory and shocked the world with his theory that the earth is a moving planet and that its motions affect other heavenly bodies.

In Saint John's Church in Thorn hangs a picture of the great astronomer. Beneath the picture is Copernicus's confession of faith:

I do not ask the grace which thou didst give Saint Paul; nor can I dare to ask the grace which thou didst grant to Saint Peter; but, the mercy which thou didst show to the Dying Robber, that mercy show to me.

Handicaps

Some of history's most successful people have succeeded in spite of handicaps.

Charles Spurgeon, perhaps the greatest preacher since Paul, was refused admittance to the University of Cambridge. But studying on his own, Spurgeon developed such biblical skills that his sermons were published weekly for forty years, selling 150 million copies in Europe and America. In addition to all this, Spurgeon wrote 135 books.

In spite of his blindness, John Milton wrote *Paradise Lost* and *Paradise Regained*. Beethoven, at forty-two, lost his hearing. But he continued to write deathless music.

Abraham Lincoln, the sixteenth president, had less than one year of formal schooling. But when he signed the Emancipation Proclamation, he set four million black slaves free.

Author Thomas Gray had a melancholic temperament and once wrote that "low spirits are my true and faithful companions." But he succeeded in spite of his melancholy.

Cervantes started *Don Quixote* while he was a prisoner. John Bunyan wrote *The Pilgrim's Progress* while he was in Bedford Jail. And the apostle Paul wrote one third of his New Testament Epistles while he was a Roman prisoner.

William Wilberforce carried on a relentless attack against the British slave trade. Sick and under a doctor's care for twenty years, he took just enough opium to keep going. He had the courage never to increase the dosage.

An outstanding Englishman who went one day to hear Wilberforce speak later said: "I saw what seemed a mere shrimp mount upon the table; but, as I listened, he grew until the shrimp became a whale." He succeeded in spite of his problems.

Victor Hugo, France's most popular literary figure, was exiled by Emperor Napoleon III for his political beliefs. Everyone thought it was the end of Hugo, but during his exile he wrote *Les Miserables* which was published simultaneously in ten languages.

If we succeed in life, most of us will have to do it in spite of some things.

Either we will handle our handicaps, or they will handle us.

When Beethoven was threatened with deafness, the most terrible crisis a musician can face, he said, "I will take life by the throat."

When Sir Walter Scott was faced with ruin because of his publisher's bankruptcy, Scott said: "No man will say 'Poor fellow' to me; my own right hand will pay the debt."

When William Booth, founder of the Salvation Army, was told that he was facing blindness, the old soldier of the cross responded: "I have used my sight for Jesus; now I'll use my blindness for Jesus!"

It is impossible to estimate the contribution the old McGuffey Reader made to American history. In that reader, as some of you may remember, is the story of the old clock that counted how many times it would have to tick in the year to come.

When the clock finally totaled the astronomical number of 31,560,000 ticks that it would have to make during the next 365 days, it gave up! It just quit.

However, when it was explained to the clock that all it had to do was make one tick at a time, it regained its morale and started up again.

When things can't get any worse, we can quit and cry, "It's impossible!" Or, we can decide that we won't quit.

The choice is up to us. We can handle our handicaps or be handled by them.[†]

Happiness

Dr. Norman Vincent Peale relates that once, while traveling on a train, he went into the diner for breakfast.

The waiter seated Dr. Peale across the table from a man and his wife who were strangers to Peale. But as Peale and the husband were talking, the man's wife suddenly blurted out, "This grapefruit is so bitter it isn't fit to eat."

In just a few minutes, the wife interrupted the conversation again: "There is a terrible draft in here," she complained.

It wasn't very long until she interrupted the third time, complaining about something else.

"You musn't let my wife disturb you," the husband said to Dr. Peale, "for she is really a very fine person. In fact, she is very clever. She is a manufacturer."

Peale was astonished that the unassuming woman was a manufacturer, so he asked, "And what does she manufacture?"

Pleasantly, still smiling, the husband replied, "She manufactures her own unhappiness."

Abraham Lincoln once observed that it had been his experience that most people were about as happy as they wanted to be.

Life is determined not so much by what it brings to us, but by what we bring to it.

> Two men looked through the self-same bars:
> One sees mud, the other sees stars.

Lord Byron and Sir Walter Scott were contemporaries. Scott, born in Edinburgh, Scotland, was seventeen years older than London-born Byron.

Both men were lame. As a baby, Scott had a bone disease that left him with a limp. Byron was born with a clubfoot. Because of their physical problems, neither boy was as athletically active as he wanted to be.

But Scott apparently handled his problem better than did Byron.

Scott seemed not to grieve over his lameness. He apparently adjusted to it, for even his closest friends said they never heard Scott complain about his problem.

Byron, on the other hand, seemed never to adjust to his clubfoot. Brooding over his lameness, he spoke frequently and bitterly about it. This may be one of the factors that contributed to his jaded, somber, and joyless writings.

Scott once received a letter from his friend Byron which contained this telling sentence: "Ah, Scott, I would give all my fame to have your happiness."

In many ways, Byron succeeded brilliantly. His *Childe Harold's Pilgrimage*, written in 1812, brought him enormous success. For three years he was toasted by all of London. As he said, he awoke one morning and found himself famous.

But by his own sad confession, Byron would have traded all his fame for happiness.

Count Lev Nikolaevich Tolstoy found that things don't bring happiness.

One of the greatest writers in history, Count Tolstoy may have been Russia's greatest writer of fiction. Some suggest that his *War and Peace* may have been the greatest work of fiction ever to come out of Russia, and others say that his *Anna Karenina* is one of the greatest love stories ever written.

Rich, famous, and the descendant of an honored family,

Tolstoy seemed to have everything. Still he was unhappy. Although he had tried everything—moral and immoral—yet he had not found happiness.

Depressed from his futile search for personal satisfaction, Tolstoy was sorely tempted to take his own life. He kept a coil of rope in his room to be used as a fire escape, but at night he would put the rope in a closet and give the key to a friend lest his temptation toward suicide be more than he could handle.

But as Tolstoy pursued his habit of taking long walks in the woods and fields of his native Russia, he noticed a strange thing. The Russian peasants had a peace and happiness that were foreign to him.

There, Tolstoy found his answer. Setting out to find God, he said, God came to him one day as he sat in the woods and delivered him from a great burden. He said he felt so happy that he wanted to jump and skip and run and that a deep song welled up in his heart.

Surely, the greatest thing Tolstoy wrote was not his masterful *War and Peace* or his lovely *Anna Karenina* but this: "To know God is to live."

Harmony

Joseph Hofmann, a Polish-American pianist and composer, died in 1957. Hofmann's musical talents are still appreciated by music authorities.

Once needing to rest, Hofmann checked into a Switzerland hotel, and there he met a mother and her young daughter. Every day after lunch, much to the discomfort of the other guests, the mother would take the little girl into the hotel's lounge where she would bang away at the piano for half an hour.

The guests were too polite to complain of the discordant sounds created by the little girl, but her raucous concert each afternoon soon emptied the lounge.

One day, however, after the other guests had fled from the racket, they were just as quickly drawn back by the beautiful music that wafted from the room out on to the still mountain air.

Returning to the room, the guests were startled to see Hofmann sitting next to the little girl. As she banged away at the keys Hofmann wove his masterful music around her discordant notes, thrilling the audience with some of the most beautiful melodies they had ever heard.

When the audience began to clap at the end of the presentation, Hofmann replied that it was the little girl they needed to thank, not him.

Is this not what Jesus does? Taking lives that are out of harmony with God, he weaves the melody of grace around our sinful, shameful lives and brings forth spiritual harmony of exquisite beauty.

Heaven

In his story titled "The Mansion" Henry van Dyke, an American Presbyterian minister and writer who died in 1933, told about a Christian dying and going to heaven. When he asked the welcoming angel to be shown the mansion that had been prepared for him, the angel told him that there was none.

Surprised, he asked why; and the angel replied, "Well, you see, we make the mansions out of material people send us from the earth, their good deeds, their spiritual power, and you have not sent us any building material."

William Makepeace Thackeray, the nineteenth-century British novelist, wrote a novel entitled *The Newcomes*. The novel was published in 1855.

Colonel Newcome, a kind-hearted soldier and an old-fashioned gentleman, lost his fortune and died in an almshouse.

But before the colonel died, Thackeray showed him in bed with his hands outside the bedcovers. The fingers were gently moving, beating time to the nearby chapel bell ringing the evening hours.

As the bell struck its last sound, Newcome's face lighted up and a smile played across his lips. Lifting his head just a little from the snowy pillow, he feebly said, *"Adsum,"* and fell back dead.

It is a Latin word which means "present." It was the word Newcome and his school friends had used when they were children, and the roll was being called at school.

Although the colonel was old and feeble, he again had the heart of a child; as he heard the Master calling the heavenly roll, he answered "*Adsum,*" as his name was called.

The day will come when the roll will be called up yonder for each of us who is a believer. When the eternal bell tolls, God help us to be ready and to answer, "Present," as our name is called.

Hope

In 1809, Napoleon was on center stage. Most of the world either hated or loved Napoleon. For five years, he had bathed Europe in its own blood. But within another five years, the Duke of Wellington had put an end to Napoleon's infamous marches when the Duke defeated Napoleon at Waterloo, Belgium.

Although the people didn't know it, even when the hour was the darkest God was still at work. For in 1809, as Napoleon swept with lightning speed across Europe, some babies were born who were destined to change history. Among them were Frederic Chopin, one of the world's leading composers, and William Gladstone, six years prime minister of Great Britain.

Also, in 1809 were born Oliver Wendell Holmes, an American author and physician, Edward Fitzgerald, the translator of *The Rubaiyat of Omar Khayyam*, and Abraham Lincoln, the great emancipator.

The masterful German composer Felix Mendelssohn and Edgar Allan Poe, author of *The Raven* and *The Pit and the Pendulum*, were also born in 1809.

Among the other babies of hope born in one of the darkest hours in history were Alfred Tennyson, England's great poet laureate, and Cyrus B. McCormack, the inventor of the reaper.

Often, when life is at its worst, God is at His best.

One of the greatest musicals ever produced was Rodgers and Hammerstein's *South Pacific*.

Shortly after the atomic bombs had been dropped on Japan at

the close of World War II, the musical swept a war-weary world with a fresh breeze of hope. It spoke of a hope that couldn't be removed from the heart.

Jesus doesn't want us to get hope out of our hearts. It is He who has put it there. The word appears in the Bible nearly 140 times.

Hope is one of the most important words in Scripture. It is such an important word that we ought to lock it up in our hearts.

Humility

Dr. B. H. Carroll was one of God's greatest Christian ministers. A veteran of the Civil War, he was wounded in battle at Mansfield, Louisiana. Shortly after his return home, Carroll was converted.

Surrendering to God's call to the ministry, Carroll became pastor of the great First Baptist Church of Waco, Texas, served as president of Baylor University, and was founder of Fort Worth's Southwestern Baptist Theological Seminary, the largest evangelical seminary in the world.

One cold, rainy, muddy night when Carroll was pastor of the Waco church, someone knocked on his front door. When Carroll went to the door, he found a preacher friend standing there. The pastor of a small country church, the preacher brother had been overtaken by the storm as he was traveling. He had come to the Carroll home hoping to spend the night.

After Dr. Carroll had visited with his friend for awhile, he escorted the visitor to the room where the traveler would spend the night. After he was certain his guest was soundly asleep, Carroll tiptoed back into the room, picked up the preacher's wet and muddy boots, cleaned and polished them, and put them back by the side of the bed.

Following the example of his servant Master, Carroll humbly ministered in Jesus' name to one whose name is not even remembered.

Incarnation

In the very heart of London is a place known as Trafalgar Square. A memorial to England's greatest naval hero, Admiral Lord Horatio Nelson, it memorializes the Battle of Trafalgar off Spain's southern coast. There, on October 21, 1805, the British fleet under Nelson defeated the French and Spanish fleet.

Although it was one of the greatest naval battles in history and gave England undisputed control of the sea, Nelson was wounded and died during the battle. Brought back to London, he was buried in the crypt of Saint Paul's Cathedral.

In the middle of Trafalgar Square stands a tall column with a giant statue of Admiral Nelson atop it. But Nelson is so high above the passersby that his features are indiscernible from the pavement below.

But in 1948, someone did something about it. An exact replica of Lord Nelson was placed at eye level where it could be examined and appreciated by the people walking through Trafalgar Square. They brought Nelson down from his colossal column where the common man and woman in the streets could see and know him.

This is what the incarnation did for us. When Jesus Christ was born of the virgin in Bethlehem, God came down to walk among men that we might see Him, know Him, and love Him.

Influence

A pamphlet by Alfred Boegner influenced Albert Schweitzer to leave Paris for the Congo.

Late one night, Schweitzer came home from the university where he was a professor. He was so exhausted he only carelessly flipped through his mail which his housekeeper had placed on his desk. Anxious to be done with the mail so he could go to bed, Schweitzer paid little attention to the mail until a magazine with a green cover caught his attention. Flipping through the magazine to see what it contained, Schweitzer was captivated by an article written by Alfred Boegner titled "The Needs of the Congo Mission."

"As I sit here in Africa," Boegner wrote, "it is my prayer that the eyes of someone on whom the eye of God has already fallen will read and answer the call and say, 'Here am I.'"

Moved by Boegner's earnest appeal for someone to come to the Congo and help him, Schweitzer bowed his head late that night and prayed, "My search is ended. I am coming."

Thus inspired to become a medical missionary, Schweitzer studied medicine from 1905 to 1913 at the University of Strasbourg. And in 1913, he sailed for Africa where he began serving at Lambarene in French Equatorial Africa; his first jungle hospital was a chicken coop.

When he made his decision to become a medical missionary, Schweitzer was principal of Saint Thomas Theological College at the University of Strasbourg. He was an author, a theologian, and the pastor of a church. Also, he was the greatest living organ interpreter of the works of Sebastian Bach. But sensing the call of God, Schweitzer turned his back on all the prestige and promise that were his and buried his life in darkest Africa.

Schweitzer's lifetime of sacrificial service in the name of Jesus Christ had its beginning because of an article by an unknown missionary in the Congo.

There is nothing more powerful than influence. One can't taste it, see it, or handle it, but it is always there, doing its quiet work.

Socrates, the Greek philosopher, never wrote a book and left behind not a single sentence from his pen so far as we know. All we know about Socrates is what others wrote about him. But his influence is still strong and vital today, centuries after he lived.

Aristotle taught a young man named Alexander to reason logically. Alexander's mother, Olympias, an ambitious and strong woman, put fire in young Alexander's spirit. With both logic and fire driving him, Alexander the Great marched out of Macedonia at the age of twenty-two and conquered the civilized world within ten years.

A little-known woman published a book in 1852 by the strange-sounding title *Uncle Tom's Cabin*. But Harriet Beecher Stowe's book broke like a thunderstorm over America and was the chief contribution of literature to the antislavery movement. No one can estimate the influence of Harriet Beecher Stowe whose book was translated into twenty-five languages.

One of James Whitcomb Riley's schoolmates called him "the most celebrated failure in arithmetic in the country." But when a sensitive teacher got hold of Riley, she saw in him a flair for literature and developed it. Her influence upon Riley helped to make him one of America's most celebrated poets.

Tchaikovsky once said that he devoted his life to music because of Mozart. "It is thanks to Mozart," Tschaikovsky wrote, "that I have devoted my life to music."

Charles Jennens took some lines he wanted to set to music to George Frederick Handel. But Handel wasn't home, so Jennens left the material, requesting Handel to help him.

When Handel found Jennens's material, he sat down to look it over. Then without stopping to eat or sleep, the inspired Handel wrote the *Messiah*, the greatest oratorio ever penned. After he had finished the exhaustive task, Handel fell on his bed and slept for seventeen hours.

Who can evaluate the influence that Jennens had on Handel or that Handel had on the world when, together, they created the greatest piece of music ever written?

Two young bicycle repairmen in Dayton, Ohio, dreamed of flying. Checking out a book from the Dayton Public Library on the life and works of a German named Lilienthal, who had succeeded in flying a glider, Orville and Wilbur Wright explored the possibilities of heavier-than-air flight. Almost everybody knows that in 1903 their dream became a reality when they flew for the first time at Kitty Hawk, North Carolina, and launched the space age. But it was the influence of Lilienthal, and others, who inspired the Wright brothers to try the impossible.

We must never minimize the power of influence for either good or evil. Fire will not burn it; water will not drown it; time will not erode it. It is eternal. Long after we are gone, our influence shall continue to live.

Josiah Elliott was a humble country preacher from North Carolina. For nearly fifty years he served God faithfully in country pastorates.

But Elliott wanted to be the pastor of a church in the city just one time during his ministry. Often he prayed, "Lord, don't keep me in the country. Please let me have just one city church."

Elliott never got his city church, but God still blessed his ministry. Out of his country churches came two young men who later became presidents of the Southern Baptist Convention. And one of the men went on to become president of the Baptist World Alliance.

One of the young men was Casper C. Warren, an outstanding preacher who served the great First Baptist Church of Tulsa, Oklahoma. The other was George W. Truett, for forty-seven years pastor of the First Baptist Church of Dallas, one of the largest Baptist churches in the world.

These two men touched the lives of millions of people.

Perhaps Josiah Elliott had a far greater ministry in his country churches than he could ever have had in the city.

Virginian Robert E. Lee, commander of the Confederate army in the Civil War, was a fine Christian gentleman. Lee was from one of the most distinguished families in America. His father, known as "Light-Horse Harry," was one of the speakers at the funeral service for George Washington.

Only 5 feet 10½ inches tall, Lee was a moral and spiritual giant. *Duty,* said Lee, was the sublimest word in the English language.

One of Lee's sons, George Washington Custis, named after Lee's mother, Mary Ann Randolph, Mary Washington's great-granddaughter, was walking with his father one day at Arlington when Custis was only a little boy. As they walked through the heavy snow, Custis walked behind his father trying to step in his father's footsteps.

Custis called out to his father. Lee turned around, and the little boy told him that he was trying to walk in his steps.

Lee said he never got away from the impression that suddenly seized him: the boy was walking in his footsteps, so he needed to be careful how he walked.

Nothing we possess is more important than our influence.[†]

Inspiration

Dr. George Washington Carver, the son of an unknown father, was born a slave. Born on a farm near Diamond Grove, Missouri, he and his mother were stolen by night riders. He was traded for a racehorse and brought back to his master, but his mother was never found.

As a young boy, he longed for an education. Although he was permitted to carry his young white master's books to the schoolhouse, he wasn't allowed inside.

But his opportunity finally came, and he entered Simpson College in Indianola, Iowa. Taking in laundry and working as a cook and janitor, Carver worked his way through college and was graduated in 1894. In 1896, he became professor at Tuskegee Institute in Alabama and spent the remainder of his life there.

God was with this little black man. He probably did more for Southern agriculture than any man who ever lived. Seeing that cotton had depleted the soil of the South, he advised Southern planters to plant peanuts and sweet potatoes. When these products flooded the market and prices fell, Carver broke the peanut and sweet potato down into three hundred usable, salable products.

Carver claimed he got his inspiration directly from heaven. Rising at four in the morning, he made it a habit to walk and pray for two hours each morning. He would then go to his laboratory and pray that God would help him to find something new and usable in the peanut.

When asked once about the secret of his success, Carver confessed that he never took books into his laboratory. God was his source of inspiration, Carver said.

It was God who drew the curtains aside and revealed His secrets, Carver confessed.

Franz Joseph Haydn was the greatest musical composer of his era. Born in Austria in 1732, Haydn was a devout Roman Catholic who began every day on his knees.

Each time Haydn was asked where he got his musical inspiration, he always responded that it came from God.

When the music did not come, Haydn said, he knew that something was blocking the divine inspiration. "Then I prayed once more for grace," he humbly confessed.

When *The Creation*, perhaps Haydn's greatest work, premiered in Vienna, he went to the presentation although he was sick and advanced in years.

After the performance, the distinguished congregation stood and gave Haydn a thunderous ovation. Finally, Haydn feebly arose to acknowledge the gratitude of his admirers.

When quietness settled over the large auditorium, Haydn humbly responded: "It all came from above."[†]

Edwin Markham, an American poet born in Oregon City, Oregon, in 1852, died in 1940. Markham won recognition with his poem "The Man with the Hoe."

Markham said his poem "The Man with the Hoe" came after seeing Jean Francoise Millet's painting of *The Man with the Hoe* in San Francisco.

Markham couldn't get the striking painting out of his mind. For weeks, he turned it over and over in his mind and then put his inspiration down on paper.

"It was handed down to me from above," he said. "I merely

lent my soul and my hand to some spiritual power over and
beyond me. I felt as if some vast hand was reaching over my
shoulder and guiding my fingers as I wrote. I gave myself over
to that hand, that inspiration, or whatever you wish to call it,
and the poem came."

Jesus

Have you ever wondered what Jesus looked like? The Bible says a lot about Him, but it doesn't tell us about the color of His hair and eyes, His height, or His weight.

Whether it is a myth or a fact, we do not know. But twenty centuries ago, it is reported, a man by the name of Publius Lentulus wrote a letter to the Roman Senate. In that letter, he gave the following description of Jesus:

> A man of stature somewhat tall; his hair the color of a chestnut fully ripe, plain to the ears, whence downward it is more orient, curling and waving about his shoulders; in the midst of his forehead is a stream or partition of his hair; forehead plain and delicate; his face without spot or wrinkle, a lovely red; his nose and mouth so forked as nothing can be represented; his beard thick, in color like his hair—not very long; his eyes, quick and clear.

Is this an actual word picture of Jesus? Or is it a fabrication of someone's imagination?

There is no way to tell. But it is interesting to read what Publius Lentulus wrote about Him.

Life

The brevity of life is written on every page of history.

Thomas Carlyle, famous Scottish historian, wrote the Savior's words "Cometh night" on the flyleaf of his first book.

Noted Scottish preacher Robert Murray McCheyne sealed his letters with Jesus' words "Cometh night."

English author Dr. Samuel Johnson, to be sure he remembered that time flies, inscribed the Lord's words "Cometh night" on his watch.

Sir Walter Scott, Scotland's greatest romantic novelist, had the words "Cometh night" sculpted on the sundial of his cottage home.

When poor Raphael was carried into his studio to take a last look at his majestic painting *The Transformation*, he sighed, "Alas, it shall never be completed!" When he was buried, the half-finished masterpiece was carried in his funeral procession.

At Abbotsford, the home of Sir Walter Scott, visitors can see Scott's last words in his journal: "Tomorrow we shall . . ." The sentence was never finished.

Franz Schubert was working on his *Unfinished Symphony* when the end came.

Frank Grasso, late conductor of the Tampa, Florida, Symphonette Orchestra, died as he was directing Schubert's *Unfinished Symphony.*

Charles Dickens, whose imaginative pen has thrilled generations, was touched by the angel of death as he laid down his pen in the middle of his novel *The Mystery of Edwin Drood*.

Robert Louis Stevenson was working on his book *Weir of Hermiston* when he died. And his last sentence, "Uncompleted," written on the morning he died stands as mute testimony to life's brevity.

Sir Walter Scott was in the midst of writing *The Seige of Malta* when he died. Joseph Conrad was writing *Suspense*, perhaps his most promising novel, when he was called away by death.

When Elizabeth I lay on her deathbed, so it is said, her last words were: "Time! Time! Give me one more moment of time! I would give my kingdom and all I possess for one more moment of time!"

Life is brief, at best. Therefore, we must make the most of the day God has given to us.

A cartoon appeared in a newspaper one New Year's Day. There was old Father Time, weary and stooped, seated behind his desk. And on the wall behind Father Time was a calendar.

Sitting in front of Father Time was an immature, ego-centered looking young fellow, pointing to the entire calendar and saying demandingly, "I'll take that one!"

Instead of giving him the whole calendar of 365 sheets, wise old Father Time carefully tore off January 1 and handed it to the young fellow. "Son," he said, "you will only take this one. Come back tomorrow, and I will give you the next one."

God intends us to live only one day at a time. Even Almighty God suggests we come back tomorrow for the next one.

One of television's best-known personalities in this decade was Eric Sevareid. For years, Sevareid was the anchorman of the ABC evening news.

Sevareid relates that when he was seventeen years old, he and a friend decided to travel from Minneapolis to York Factory via the Hudson River. It was a long and difficult journey, Sevareid said, but the last leg of the journey was the most difficult and dangerous. That part of their trek stretched 450 miles across a rugged wilderness where there was only one settlement. He and his friend were frightened at the thought of making the last leg of the journey all by themselves.

An old fur trader, however, gave them some good advice just as they were about to leave on the last leg of their odyssey. "Boys," he said, "just think about the next mile you will have to go. Don't think about all those other miles. Never think about the 450 miles that lie ahead of you. Only think of the next mile."

Many years after that unforgettable journey, when Sevareid's hair had turned a silvery gray, he commented on the good advice that the wise old man had given to them.

"Many times in the future," Sevareid said, "I was to rediscover that there is only one mile to make, never 450."

Life must be lived one day at a time. At the beginning of each new year, although there is a calendar with 12 months and 365 days, God gives our days only one at a time. And that is the way life must be lived.

Little Things

It's human nature to worship at the biggest altars. But what about the little things? Are they not also important?

One vote gave Oliver Cromwell control of England in 1656.

One vote changed France from a monarchy to a republic in 1875.

One vote denied Aaron Burr the presidency.

One vote elected Thomas Jefferson to that office.

Blinded by bigness, we earthlings often miss the importance of little things.

But Jesus didn't. He spoke of the Father attending the funeral of one sparrow that falls. And it was one sheep the Good Shepherd sought until He found it.

Jesus knew the importance of little things. And it is a lesson we need to learn, for life's sweetest symphonies are often played in the minor keys.[†]

Love

Many years ago when the Roman Empire was spreading throughout the world, King Tigranes of Armenia was taken captive. Standing before the conquering Roman general waiting for the death sentence to be passed, Tigranes fell upon his knees before the general and pleaded for his family. "Do with me what you like," he said, "but I beg you to spare my family."

As they left the general, King Tigranes asked his wife what she thought about the general. And she replied, "I never saw him."

"But what do you mean 'you never saw him'?" Tigranes asked. "You were standing within a few feet of him. You could not help but see him. What were you looking at?"

With tears now sparkling in her eyes, the queen gently replied to her beloved husband: "I saw no one but you. My eyes only saw the one who was willing to die for me."

This, surely, is the attitude of every believer toward his Lord and Savior, Jesus Christ.

A monk of the Middle Ages, loved and respected by his people, announced that on a particular evening he would preach a sermon on the love of God.

When the time for the service came, the cathedral was packed to capacity; and the people stood silently, waiting for their beloved teacher.

As evening set in and the last rays of light faded from the sky, the monk lighted a candle and walked up to the life-size statue of Christ hanging on the cross.

Without saying a word, the monk held the candle before the

nail-pierced hands. He then showed the people the wound in the Savior's side and lifted the candle high so they could see the thorns on His brow.

The monk then returned the candle to its place and left the cathedral.

Not a word was spoken, but the people never forgot the monk's sermon on the love of God.

In her biography of Howard Thurman, Elizabeth Yates tells about a visit Dr. Thurman made to India.

A poor little Indian boy from one of the villages heard the missionary preach. After Dr. and Mrs. Thurman had gone to bed that night, there was a timid knock at their door. Opening the door they saw a boy standing there, wearing the clothing of one of India's untouchables.

"I listened to you today," the little boy said, "and I want to ask you, 'Can you give hope to a nobody?'"

There are no "nobodies" to God. Each of us is a somebody of infinite worth.

You are so important to God that Jesus Christ died to save you (John 3:16).

Dr. Herschel Hobbs, a former president of the Southern Baptist Convention, said that his father died when Hobbs was nine years old.

It was 1917, and because of the war it was impossible to hire someone to help them on their farm. Hobb's mother would plow the first furrow, laying out the rows for young Herschel to follow. She would then turn the plow over to her son. It was hard work, and the family faced hard times.

However, early one morning, the Hobbses looked down the road and saw a sight that deeply moved them. Wagons were moving toward their farm. The neighbors, for miles around, were coming to the rescue. By the time night fell on their forty-acre farm, the ground was plowed, and the crop was planted.

Love did it. Christian love always finds a way to express itself. It is never idle. Although it may not say much, Christian love is always busy.[†]

Man

British author H. G. Wells was born in 1866 and died in 1946. Among his well-known works are *The Invisible Man* and *The War of the Worlds*.

In one of his stories titled *The Soul of a Bishop*, Wells shows that a man can never know everything there is to know about God.

A bishop and an angel were talking. The angel told the bishop that none of men's religions clearly understand God—that they teach more about Him than they clearly understand.

Hoping that the angel would give him some special revelation about the Almighty, Wells had the bishop say to the angel, "But the truth, you can tell me the truth."

Smiling, the angel lovingly stroked the bald spot on the bishop's head. Holding the bishop's head firmly in his hands, the angel said: "Truth! Yes, I could tell you. But could this hold it? Not this little box of brains. You haven't things to hold it with inside this."

If finite man could understand all about the infinite God, God would not be much of a God. Man can understand some things about God, but the rest he has to take on faith.

Miracles

John Witherspoon, a member of the American Continental Congress and a signer of the Declaration of Independence, was also a Presbyterian minister.

He came to America in 1768 to become president of the College of New Jersey, now Princeton University.

Witherspoon lived two miles from the college campus at a place called Rocky Hill. Each day, Witherspoon would drive his buggy the two miles into the college campus.

One day, as he was in his study at the school, a neighbor rushed in and excitedly exclaimed that God had spared his life as he was riding into town. He told his friend Witherspoon that the horse had run away, and the buggy had been wrecked, but he had been delivered unharmed. And he asked Witherspoon to join him in a prayer of thanksgiving for his miraculous deliverance.

But Witherspoon wasn't as touched as his neighbor had expected him to be. "Let me tell you something more marvelous than your miracle," Witherspoon said. "I make that same two-mile journey every day and have done it hundreds of times, and not one time did my horse leave the pathway, and not one time has my buggy turned over. Many times, I have traveled it," he said, "and I have never been hurt."

Missions

William Carey, the father of modern missions, was born in Northamptonshire, England, in 1761.

An apprentice shoemaker at fourteen, Carey was converted in a small Baptist church and began to preach at eighteen.

Carey made his commitment to Jesus as a result of the influence of a young, fellow cobbler who worked by Carey's side. In later life, Carey said about his friend: he couldn't answer all of my questions, and I couldn't answer his life.

Seizing every spare minute to read widely, young Carey mastered Latin, Greek, Hebrew, French, and Dutch. He also acquired a knowledge of botany and zoology.

When a copy of Captain Cook's *Voyages Around the World* fell into Carey's hands, his vision was lifted beyond his native England to distant lands. Hanging a map of the world in his cobbler's stall, Carey collected information about those distant lands, and there began to burn in his heart the desire to carry the gospel to them.

Once Carey attended a ministerial meeting in Nottingham, and the moderator asked if anyone had a subject he would like to present for discussion. Carey proposed they discuss "the duty of Christians to attempt the spread of the gospel among the heathen nations."

Revealing the antagonism of that era to missionary work, the moderator rose and rebuked Carey: "Young man, sit down. When God pleases to convert the heathen, he will do it without your aid or mine."

But Carey's love for missions would not die. On May 31, 1792, the modern mission movement was born as Carey preached his now-famous sermon, based on Isaiah 54:2, in which he made two profound statements: "Expect great things from God," and "Attempt great things for God."

Shortly after he preached his message, twelve committed

ministers met at Kettering and formed the first Baptist Missionary Society. And Carey was the first to offer himself for missionary service.

One year later, in June 1793, Carey set sail for India on a Danish vessel, landing at Calcutta five months later. As he departed England, his last message to his friends at home was this: "Yonder in India is a gold mine. I will descend and dig, but you at home must hold the ropes."

The modern mission movement had begun. And Carey's influence was destined to be felt around the world and to the end of time.

William Carey, the first modern missionary to a foreign land, landed at Calcutta, India, in 1793. He was there nearly twenty years before Ann and Adoniram Judson left America to be foreign missionaries. Influenced toward missions as they read the life of William Carey, they set sail from America in 1812.

Visiting Carey in Serampore, India, they walked through his beautiful garden and talked to him about his missionary service.

Three attempts had been made on Carey's life. A fire had killed five co-workers at his mission. His printing house and translations of the Bible on which he had been working were all destroyed. The Judsons wanted to know how Carey had been able to stay, facing such adversities.

When Young Ann Judson who, herself, was destined to die on the mission field asked Carey how he could carry on, Carey replied, "Oh, it was through the grace of God . . . let me show you the path to my strength."

He then led the Judson's to a quiet garden place and reverently said: "I come here at five o'clock in the morning to pray aloud, talking to God and listening to him amid these flowers that he created in all their beauty. I leave the garden about six o'clock for my breakfast and to begin my work for the day. After supper, I come again for prayer and meditation, with my Bible in my hand."

Carey's work was monumental. Under his supervision the Bible, in whole or in part, was translated in more than thirty-five languages and dialects. He also compiled grammars in Sanskrit, Bengali, Marathi, Telugu, and Sikh languages, to mention only a few of his literary accomplishments.

In 1832, Carey completed the eighth edition of the Bengali New Testament. "My work is done," he said. "I have nothing more to do but to wait the will of God."

Carey died on June 9, 1834, having served Christ in India forty-one years. On his tombstone at Serampore is the epitaph which he wrote for himself: "A poor wretched worm. On thy kind arms I fall."

David Brainerd was born in Massachusetts in 1718. Although he lived only twenty-nine years, young Brainerd walked with God.

Brainerd was a missionary to the Indians along the Hudson and Delaware rivers in early-day America. Although he preached only three or four years, Brainerd served God in an unusual way.

When young William Carey in England read about David Brainerd's life of hardship as a missionary to the Indians, Brainerd's influence moved Carey toward India.

Robert Murray McCheyne also read young Brainerd's biography, and it led him into the ministry in his native Scotland. Although McCheyne died before he was thirty, he is regarded as one of Christendom's greatest preachers.

Jonathan Edwards was also touched by Brainerd. He was Brainerd's father-in-law, and he watched the young preacher die. Later, he said: "I praise God that in his providence, Brainerd should die in my house so that I might hear his prayers, so that I might witness his consecration and be inspired by his example."

Fifteen years older than Brainerd, Jonathan Edwards was profoundly influenced by Brainerd. Edwards later became president of what is now Princeton University, and he was also recognized as the greatest preacher of America's colonial era.

John Wesley, the founder of Methodism, was also deeply affected by Brainerd. Even as Brainerd was dying in Massachusetts, Wesley was preaching at a conference in England and asking his listeners what could be done to revive the Lord's work in England.

Then answering his own question, Wesley said: "That every preacher read carefully the life of David Brainerd."

Money

When oilman John Paul Getty died, it was estimated that his estate was worth from $2 billion to $4 billion. And it is estimated that Howard Hughes left an estate worth more than $2 billion.

How much is a billion dollars? Well, it's a one with nine zeros after it. And if you had spent $1,000 a day since the day that Jesus Christ was born, you would not yet be broke!

But let's go a step further. How much is a trillion dollars? Well, a trillion dollars is a one with twelve zeros after it. It is a billion dollars multiplied by 1,000 or a million dollars multiplied by a million.

If you laid one trillion one-dollar bills end to end, they would make 200 round trips to the moon.

If you stacked one trillion one-dollar bills on top of each other, the stack would be 67,866 miles high.

If you had a trillion silver dollars, they would weigh more than 29 million tons—more than 350 *Queen Elizabeth* steamships.

If you were to count your trillion dollars, and counted at the rate of $10,000 a minute and worked at it eight hours a day, six days a week, it would take you 667 years to count your money.

If you had a trillion dollars and had begun spending $1 million a day since the day Jesus was born, you still wouldn't be broke. You could continue to live that lavishly for the next 757 years.

Concerning the acquiring and grasping of wealth, Jesus asked two sobering questions in Mark 8:36-37: "For what shall it profit a man, if he shall gain the whole world, and lose his own soul? Or what shall a man give in exchange for his soul?"

Jesus told us that, after all, there is something vastly more important than the acquiring of wealth.

Mother

Sir James M. Barrie, a Scottish writer and the author of *Peter Pan*, was born in Kirriemuir, Scotland, in 1860. Knighted in London in 1913, Barrie also served as director of Saint Andrews University from 1919 to 1922. He died in 1937.

Barrie wrote plays and novels. His best-known play, *Peter Pan*, has been performed around the world.

The most influential personality in Barrie's life, apparently, was his mother. In a biography about her titled *Margaret Ogilvie*, Barrie magnified the inner strength of this Scotswoman.

He described the day his mother's oldest son was seriously injured in an accident. As she prepared to go to him, she received a telegram informing her that he had died.

Returning home, Mrs. Barrie accepted her grief as well as she could. Although she was a woman of strong Christian faith, she never recovered from her great sorrow. From the time of her son's tragic death until her own death, her health was never good.

In his biography about his mother, Barrie said this is how his mother got her soft face. As she wrestled with her own deep grief, it left its compassionate imprint upon her life and countenance. And, Barrie added, it was because of this that other mothers came to his own mother for comfort when they had lost a child.

All of us owe more to our dear mothers than we could ever tell. Their influence upon us is immeasurable.

John Quincy Adams said about his mother, "All that I am my mother made me."

Abraham Lincoln wrote about his mother, "All that I am or hope to be, I owe to my angel mother."

Writing about all mothers, Napoleon said, "Let France have good mothers, and she will have good sons."

Dwight L. Moody, the great evangelist, said about his mother, "All that I have ever accomplished in life, I owe to my mother."

George Washington said that his mother taught him the biblical ideals of political and social morality which Washington kept before the nation throughout his life. The Scriptures were read daily in the home of his childhood, and family prayers were offered twice daily.

The mother of President James A. Garfield was an earnest Christian. A widow, she carefully taught the Scriptures to her four children.

The mother of patriot William Penn so impressed him with the importance of faith in Christ that he took as his life's motto, "This is the victory, even our faith which overcomes the world."

Thomas Edison, history's greatest inventor, probably expressed all of our feelings about the influence of our mothers when he wrote: "I did not have my mother long, but she cast over me an influence that has lasted all my life. If it had not been for her appreciation and faith in me at a critical time in my experience, I should never have become an inventor. I was always a careless boy. But her firmness, her goodness, were potent powers to keep me in the right path. My mother was the making of me."

Mothers come in all shapes, sizes, and ages. But all are beautiful. And we owe a debt to them we shall never be able to pay.

In one of his novels, Victor Hugo dramatically described mothers, these "angels with soft faces," as Scottish author James Barrie called them.

A platoon of soldiers was passing through some woods where, just a few days before, a terrible battle had been fought. When the captain saw some nearby bushes move, he halted his troops and told the sergeant to see what was behind the bushes.

A few minutes later, the sergeant came back with a mother and two little children. They looked hungry and terribly frightened, for they had been hiding in the woods since the battle.

"Sergeant," the captain said, "give them something to eat."

Reaching into his pack, the sergeant took out a long loaf of bread and handed it to the mother. Quickly, almost desperately, she broke it into two pieces and gave a piece to each child.

As the soldiers watched the hungry children eagerly eat the bread, the sergeant asked, "Captain, can it be that she isn't hungry? Surely, she hasn't eaten for days."

Waiting a few seconds before he answered, the captin cleared his choked-up voice and softly replied: "No sergeant, it isn't because she isn't hungry. It's because she is their mother."

Nature

Human nature is like the basement Walter Murdock described in one of his essays. In his story "Beasts in the Basement," he told about the house his eccentric aunt left him when she died.

The will stipulated that he must keep alive a peculiar group of animals the aunt housed in her cellar. There was a tiger from India, which had been acquired by his grandfather; a parrot, which had belonged to his great-aunt Celina; a donkey that had been given by Uncle Henry; and other animals that had been given by deceased relatives.

Murdock had to keep the animals alive, by the terms of the will, but they were a constant embarrassment to him. Often, as he was entertaining friends, the donkey would bray, or the parrot would screech, or one of the other animals would make strange noises.

When the animals became restless, Murdock would cough, clear his throat, turn up the volume on the radio, shuffle his feet, or carry on in some other way so as to distract his guests.

It's a parable of fallen, sinful, human nature. Within each of us are drives and instincts which cannot be hidden. In our finest moments they express themselves, much to our chagrin.

The only answer to our dilemma is Jesus Christ who by his grace can give us victory over the sinful nature that controls us (2 Cor. 5:17).

Nevertheless

Sir James Simpson was a Scottish physician who discovered the anesthetic properties of chloroform. As a result, Simpson gave to a hurting world painless surgery.

His little daughter lies buried in a lonely cemetery in Edinburgh, Scotland. For her epitaph, Simpson had the words "Nevertheless, I live" carved on her headstone.

When Issen, the great Norwegian dramatist came to die, his last word was "Nevertheless."

Facing death, Jesus went into the garden to pray, and he prayed, "Nevertheless . . ."

Optimism

Thomas A. Edison was the greatest inventor in history. With less than three months of formal schooling, he had an intense desire to succeed and a determination that wouldn't quit.

When a friend tried to console Edison over ten thousand experiments that had not worked, Edison's optimistic reply was, "Why, I have not failed. I've just found ten thousand ways that won't work."

In later years, a fire destroyed his laboratory in New Jersey. A lifetime of research went up in smoke. But as the fire roared, and Edison's son came to comfort his father, Edison optimistically told his son to go get his mother.

"Tell her to come immediately," Edison commanded. "Tell her that everything has been destroyed that we might have a new start."

Missionary Adoniram Judson was lying in a foul Burmese jail. Imprisoned because of his Christian faith, Judson had thirty-two pounds of chains around his ankles; his feet were tied to a bamboo pole four feet off the ground, and the temperature was 100 degrees.

A fellow prisoner—a nonbeliever—knowing that Judson was a Christian missionary sneeringly asked: "Well, Mr. Judson, what do you think now about the prospects for the conversion of the heathen?"

Without hesitating a moment, Judson replied: "Sir, the prospects for the conversion of the heathen are as bright as the promises of God."

Judson had sufficient reason for self-pity. But even in prison, his life hanging in the balances, Judson could optimistically look forward to the future, knowing he was in the hands of Him who never forsakes His children.[†]

Persecution

When Polycarp, a second-century bishop of Smyrna, was arrested by Roman soldiers because of his Christian faith, he fed them and then asked that he might have an hour to pray before he was taken away. And he prayed with such fervency that the soldiers regretted they had to arrest him. Carried before the proconsul, Polycarp was condemned to be burned to death in the marketplace.

"Swear," the proconsul said, "and I will release thee—reproach Christ."

The old bishop answered: "Eighty and six years have I served Him, and He never once wronged me; how then shall I blaspheme my King, who hath saved me?"

The soldiers bound the old saint to a stake, stacking a large pile of wood at his feet. Usually, the Christians were nailed to their stakes, but Polycarp assured his persecutors he would not try to escape, so they only tied him with ropes.

When the fire was ignited, the flames encircled Polycarp's body without touching him. Seeing what had happened, the executioner ordered Polycarp to be pierced with a sword. But when the soldier ran his sword through Polycarp's body, so much blood flowed out that the fire was extinguished.

But the enemies of the gospel would not be defeated in their quest for Polycarp's death. They insisted that his body be taken down from the stake and burned on a pile of wood. After it was done, believers collected their bishop's bones and gave the old saint a Christian burial.

Another Christian martyr was young Hugh Mackail of Edinburgh, Scotland. A dissenter from the established church, which was a capital offense, Mackail was slain in 1666.

Sentenced to die in four days, Mackail was led away to the cell. As he passed the weeping people lining the street, there were no tears in Mackail's eyes and no trace of self-pity.

Walking along the street back to his cell, he cried out to the throngs: "Trust in God!"

Catching a glimpse of a friend in the crowd, he shouted: "Good news! Good news! I am within a four-days journey of a site of Jesus Christ!"

Faith in the Lord Jesus helps us to triumph in life's direst trials. The testimony of thousands, through the years, gives ample proof to that.

Vast numbers of people have died for the Christian faith. The first great persecution of believers began in AD 67 when Nero was emperor of Rome.

Ordering Rome to be set on fire, Nero went to the Tower of Macaenas and strummed his harp, singing the song of the burning of Troy. He said he wanted to destroy everything before he died.

The terrible fire roared for nine dreadful days. When word came to Nero that the populace was blaming him for the fiery holocaust, he shifted the blame to the Christians to excuse himself, inaugurating the first great persecution against the Christians.

He had some of the believers sewn up in the skins of wild animals and turned dogs loose on them, worrying the Christians until they died. Dressing others in shirts made stiff with wax, Nero had them tied to axletrees and set on fire to illuminate his gardens. And it was during these Neronian persecutions that both the apostles Paul and Peter were slain.

But Nero's persecution of the believers did not diminish their number or their spirit. In spite of Nero, the faith spread to all the Mediterranean world.

Perseverance

William Carey, the father of modern missions, labored seven years in India before he baptized his first convert.

Adoniram Judson labored faithfully seven years in Burma before he baptized his first convert.

Robert Morrison, a missionary to China, also labored seven years before he baptized his first Chinese convert.

Medical missionary and explorer David Livingstone served fourteen years in Africa before he witnessed his first conversion.

Adam Clark spent forty years writing his commentary on the Scriptures.

Noah Webster worked thirty-six years on his dictionary, crossing the ocean twice to collect material.

William Cullen Bryant wrote *Thanatopsis* one hundred times before he was satisfied with it.

Thomas Gray wrote *Elegy Written in a Country Churchyard* seventy-five times before he was satisfied with it.

Edward Gibbon spent twenty-six years writing his *Decline and Fall of the Roman Empire* before it was completed.

Charles Goodyear worked ten years in poverty and ridicule perfecting the rubber from which he made millions in the tire industry.

And George Stephenson worked fifteen years developing the locomotive.

Perseverance pays off!

Praise

Joni Eareckson Tada is tragically crippled as a result of a diving accident. A quadriplegic paralyzed from her shoulders down, Joni broke her neck when she dove into the shallow waters of Chesapeake Bay.

But Joni is a living testimony to the power of prayer and praise. After her accident, she became bitter and blamed God for her problems. But through prayer and Bible study, her faith in God was rekindled, and her life took on new meaning.

An accomplished artist who has developed a line of greeting cards and has completed hundreds of original drawings, Joni draws by holding the pen between her teeth.

When the Gillette Company learned that Joni used their Papermate pens with which to draw, they offered to put her on their payroll.

Beneath each of her drawings, Joni puts her name and then adds the letters *PTL*. When she is asked what the letters mean, Joni happily replies: "They mean 'Praise the Lord!'"

It opens doors for Joni. And she goes on to tell them why she is able to praise the Lord and what Jesus has done for her.

Prayer

Hudson Taylor, the founder of China Inland Mission, was born in 1853. On his way to China to serve as a missionary, the sailing vessel in which Taylor was a passenger was becalmed in the ocean.

For days, the wind didn't blow, and the vessel couldn't move. In desperation the captain, who was not a Christian, went to Mr. Taylor and said: "Mr. Taylor, I want you to pray that God will send the winds so that we can begin to move again."

Taylor said that he would be glad to pray on the condition that the captain first lift the sails. But the captain refused. "Why, my men will think that I'm crazy if I raise the sails in this calm," he retorted.

"Then," Hudson Taylor said, "I will not ask God to send the wind. If I'm going to pray for wind, I must have enough faith to raise the sails."

Only then did the missionary go below to ask the Father in heaven to send His wind. And it wasn't long until God answered Taylor's prayer, filling the sails with wind and speeding the ship on its way.

Praying isn't enough. When we pray, we must believe God will act and then step out on faith.[†]

Preparation

Abraham Lincoln was born in a backwoods cabin in Kentucky in 1809. The son of a farmer, Lincoln had less than a year of formal schooling.

Books were scarce in Lincoln's frontier home, but *Robinson Crusoe, The Pilgrim's Progress, Aesop's Fables,* and the Bible were read avidly and were absorbed quickly by his young mind.

Studying by his pine-log fire at night, practicing his arithmetic on a wooden shovel and then shaving off the figures so he could write new ones, Lincoln did the best he could. "I will study and prepare, and someday my opportunity will come," he kept saying to himself in those difficult days.

Lincoln moved with his family to Illinois in 1825. Settling on the banks of the Sangamon River, Lincoln worked with his father, clearing the land for the plow.

When Denton Offutt, a trader, moved near the Lincoln cabin, he offered nineteen-year-old Lincoln a job.

Offutt had hogs and corn that needed to be delivered to New Orleans. When he offered Lincoln and two other young fellows fifty cents a day each to float his cargo down the Mississippi, they accepted. He even promised to give each of them a bonus of twenty dollars if the cargo was delivered safely to New Orleans.

Maybe Lincoln had seen slaves before, but when he arrived in New Orleans, he saw slavery on a large scale. Then when he was thirty-one, he made another trip to the Crescent City and saw, again, the horror of the slave trade.

On one of these trips, historians are not sure which one, Lincoln determined that if he ever had the opportunity, he would do something about the abuse of black people. *If ever I get a chance to hit that thing, I'll hit it hard,* he said to himself.

Lincoln got his chance. When the Republican National Convention met in Chicago on May 16, 1860, Lincoln was nominated on the third ballet.

Leaving Springfield, Illinois, on February 11, 1861, he arrived in Washington on February 23. On March 14, 1861, Lincoln was inaugurated president. He was the sixteenth president, and he was fifty-two years old.

On January 1, 1863, Lincoln signed the document for which he is best remembered. Signing the Emancipation Proclamation, Lincoln declared that slaves "are, and henceforward shall be free."

But few slaves were freed as a result of the Emancipation Proclamation. It affected only the Confederate States where federal officers were present to enforce it. Slaves in loyal border states were not affected, although Lincoln urged the owners to set them free.

But what the Emancipation Proclamation could not accomplish because of the war, it accomplished in other ways. As a result of the Emancipation Proclamation, Amendment 13 was added to the Constitution. Adopted in December 1865, the amendment forever ended slavery in the United States.

Lincoln's preparation paid off. Although no president in the history of the United States has been more hated and more loved, Lincoln's effect on the nation was profound and undeniable.

Problems

The people who have lived the most successfully and have made the greatest contributions to life are often the ones who have had to overcome the greatest problems.

Sir Walter Scott was plagued by lameness.

George Washington learned from the cold snows of Valley Forge.

Abraham Lincoln had to deal with poverty and the lack of a formal education.

Benjamin Disraeli, the only Jew ever elected prime minister of Great Britain, had to overcome prejudice.

Theodore Roosevelt had a lifelong battle with asthma.

Thomas A. Edison, as a result of a childhood accident, was almost totally deaf.

Robert Louis Stevenson left his native Scotland for Samoa because of tuberculosis.

Helen Keller struggled against the dual handicaps of blindness and deafness.

Demosthenes, history's greatest orator, was born with a speech impediment.

William Cowper, author of "There Is a Fountain Filled with Blood," was plagued by melancholy.

Handel, whose *Messiah* is sung around the world at Christmastime, wrote it at a time of great discouragement.

John Bunyan wrote *The Pilgrim's Progress* from a jail cell.

Lou Gehrig, perhaps the greatest baseball player in history, was forever playing with broken bones in his hands.

Napoleon graduated forty-second in a class of forty-three men.

Louis Pasteur, the father of modern medicine, was called by one of his teachers "the least promising student in my calss."

Personal problems will never bar the way to success to those who are determined.

Providence

Probably, Christopher Columbus had never been more discouraged in his life. He believed that out beyond the Mediterranean and the Gates of Hercules lay a vast and unexplored world. But no one believed Columbus, and no one would finance his expedition.

One day, as Columbus was returning to Italy, he stopped at a convent not far from the old city of Grenada. Tired and thirsty, he asked a monk for a drink of water. He then told the monk of his dreams and his inability to find financing for his expedition.

The monk not only gave Columbus a glass of water, but he also intervened with Queen Isabella. The Spanish queen agreed to finance Columbus, providing fourteen thousand dollars from her treasury. And out of Columbus's request for a glass of water came the discovery of America.

France and Italy were at war, and John Calvin, on his way to Italy, had to detour through Geneva because the regular road he planned to travel was closed.

In Geneva, Calvin met Guillaume Farel, a fiery, well-known reformer, who persuaded Calvin to stay in Geneva. Working together, they ignited a political and religious reformation in Geneva which was destined to sweep the world.

Because of a closed road and a chance meeting with Farel, John Calvin became one of the foremost leaders of the Protestant Reformation in Europe in the 1500s.

A farmer and his two sons were working a frontier farm in Kentucky one day in 1784 when a shot rang out, and the farmer fell to the ground.

The elder son, seeing that his father had been shot by the Indians, ran to the nearby cabin for a gun. As he ran back toward the field, he saw his screaming, wiggling little brother being kidnapped by an Indian.

The older boy was an expert shot. He took aim, fired, the Indian fell, and the little brother fled to safety.

The little boy who was saved from the clutches of the Indian was named Thomas. He would grow up, marry, and become the father of Abraham Lincoln.

One wonders how the history of the United States would have been written during the tragic days of the Civil War if the father of Abraham Lincoln had not been spared by divine Providence.

Had it not been for divine Providence, James Garfield would never have lived to become the twentieth president of the United States.

As a teenager, Garfield worked on a canal boat named *The Evening Star*. One midnight in 1847, young Garfield was awakened out of a deep sleep for duty on deck. As he picked up a rope on deck and pulled at it, it became lodged in a crevice. Pulling harder, the rope came loose, and Garfield fell into the dark waters below.

Even as he fell overboard and sank beneath the cold, dark waters, Garfield instinctively clung to the rope. Just as he thought he would surely drown, he felt the rope become taut in his hand, and he quickly pulled himself up on deck.

After his shift on deck was over, he picked up the rope and flung it toward the crevice in which it had become entangled the night before. Five, ten, fifteen, a hundred times he threw the rope at the crevice, trying to catch it, but he never succeeded. Coiling the rope up, young Garfield came to the conclusion that his life had been spared by divine Providence.

Since God had spared his life, he reasoned, it must have been for a purpose. Quitting his job, he went back home to Ohio. Entering the door to his home, Garfield walked in on his mother who was on her knees, praying for him by name. Deeply moved, he told his mother that he had made up his mind to make something of himself and that he was going to get an education.

Garfield did make something of himself. He graduated from Williams College, and it is recorded that he was so brilliant that he could simultaneously write Greek with one hand and Latin with the other.

Entering the Union army, Garfield rose to the rank of brigadier general. He was then elected to Congress. In 1881, he was inaugurated the twentieth president of the United States.

On July 2, 1881, Garfield was in Washington's railroad station preparing to return to Williams College for the twenty-fifth reunion of his class. Suddenly, Charles J. Guiteau, a man Garfield had refused to appoint as United States consul in Paris, stepped out of the crowd and fired two shots at the president.

One bullet only grazed Garfield's arm, but the other lodged in his back. Surgeons could not find the slug with their probes, and Alexander Graham Bell, the inventor of the telephone, tried unsuccessfully to locate it with an electrical device.

Eighty days after he was shot, September 19, 1881, James A. Garfield died. But he would never have been elected president if it had not been for divine Providence that saved his life one dark night as a sixteen-year-old, working on *The Evening Star*.

On November 8, 1942, the Allied forces invaded French North Africa. And on that fateful day in history, divine Providence smiled on the Allies in a way that should never be forgotten.

During the morning hours, 150,000 United States troops and 140,000 British troops landed in a massive invasion on the African coast. Remarkably, there was very little loss of life.

The chief reason that the invasion was so successful and so few lives were lost with so many troops engaged in the battle was that the seas were calmer that night than at any time during the 25,000 days that records had been kept.

God restrained the sea and demonstrated His strength. Divine Providence worked that day for the American and British troops.

Repentance

In her book *Devotion for Personal and Group Worship,* Virginia Eli tells about two brothers who were convicted many years ago of stealing sheep. When they were caught, justice was swift, and the bothers were branded on their foreheads with the letters *ST*—"Sheep Thief."

One of the brothers could not bear the shame that was his. He moved away to a foreign land and tried to lose himself. But everywhere he went, people asked him what the initials *ST* meant. He kept on moving until finally he died, broken and bitter, far from home.

The other brother acted differently. He knew he couldn't run away and deny that he had stolen the sheep. So he decided to stay at home and live such an exemplary life that he would prove his repentance to his neighbors.

Time passed, and he lived in such a way that he regained the respect of his onetime friends. After many years, no one questioned his character and integrity. He had been an exemplary citizen.

A stranger to the community saw the man with the initials on his forehead and asked an old-timer what they meant. But the old-timer replied that he did not exactly remember the particulars, but he thought the abbreviation stood for saint.

According to the Bible, repentance is a personal act in which we turn from our sin to Jesus Christ in saving faith. Repentance is a change of heart and results in changed behavior.

David Lloyd George, prime minister of Great Britain during World War I, was taking a walk with a friend one day; each time they walked through a gate, George would close it after them.

The friend saw what he was doing. "You don't need to close those gates," the friend said. "The caretakers will do that."

"Yes, I think I do," replied George. "You see, I've spent my life shutting gates behind me. A wise person always does that. When one shuts a gate behind himself, the past is held there."

Repentance is closing gates behind us. We can't change or erase past sins, but we can shut the gate on them.

Resurrection

Thomas Jefferson, the author of the Declaration of Independence, was born on April 13, 1743, in Albermarle County, Virginia. He died on July 4, 1826, at Monticello, his Virginia home, fifty years to the day after the adoption of the Declaration of Independence.

Jefferson was a deist—one who believed in the God revealed in nature. Congress once printed a special edition of Thomas Jefferson's Bible, in which he had cut out all references to the supernatural. He confined himself solely to Christ's ethical teachings.

The closing, somber words to Jefferson's Bible are these: "There laid they Jesus, and rolled a great stone to the mouth of the sepulchre and departed."

Jefferson, unlike Benjamin Franklin who was a fellow deist, apparently did not believe in the resurrection from the dead.

The fifteenth child in a family of seventeen children, Franklin was born in Boston, Massachusetts, on January 17, 1706. At the age of eighty-four on April 17, 1790, Franklin died in Philadelphia.

Franklin wrote his own epitaph. One who visits the old cemetery of Christ's Church in Philadelphia can see Franklin's grave, but there is no trace of his epitaph. But the epitaph which he prepared for himself reads like this:

The Body
of
Benjamin Franklin
Printer
(Like the cover of an old book
Its contents Torn Out
And stript of its lettering and gilding)
Lies here, food for worms.
But the work shall not be lost
For it will (As he believed)

Appear Once More
In a new and more elegant edition
Revised and corrected
by
THE AUTHOR

In the crypt of Saint Paul's Cathedral in London, the visitor can visit the grave of Lord Horatio Nelson, England's greatest naval hero. At Trafalgar Square, in the heart of London, the victorious Nelson stands atop a colossal column.

Nelson's last battle was the sea battle at Trafalgar, off the coast of Spain. On October 21, 1805, Nelson's twenty-seven ships attacked the thirty-three warships of Napoleon's Spanish and French fleet. Wounded in the spine in the battle, Nelson lived long enough to know that victory was his. His last words were, "Thank God, I have done my duty."

When Nelson was brought back to Saint Paul's for burial, thirty trumpeters standing at the cathedral doors blew their trumpets when the dead admiral arrived. However, the sound of those trumpets did not awaken Nelson.

But what thirty trumpeters were not able to do, one trumpeter will do when Jesus comes on the resurrection morning.

In the Book of Acts alone, the apostles tell the story of the Savior's resurrection twenty-nine times. It is the only hope we have when death wraps its mantle around us.

There are two great rocks on either side of the Strait of Gibraltar, where the Mediterranean meets the Atlantic, which are called the Pillars of Hercules. The great rock on the European side is called Calpe. The Greeks called the rock on the opposite side Abyla. Mythology relates that Hercules put the rocks there when he went in search of the kingdom of Geryon.

Mythology also relates that these two rocks were bound together by a huge scroll hanging between them. On the scroll were the Latin words *Ne plus ultra*, meaning "No more beyond." It was a warning to the ancient mariners not to sail beyond the Strait of Gibraltar. The ancients thought there was nothing beyond, and to sail past Gibraltar would mean to fall off the edge of the world.

But Columbus proved them all wrong. Leaving Palos, Spain, on August 3, 1492, Columbus sailed past the Pillars of Hercules out into the broad Atlantic and on westward to discover a new world. There were ninety men, counting Columbus, and they sailed westward in three ships: the *Santa Maria*, the *Pinta*, and the *Nina*.

In spite of threatened mutiny, horrendous storms, and appalling discouragement, the men sailed on and on until at last they landed in the Bahamas on October 12.

It is said that after Columbus sailed through the Pillars of Hercules and out into the Atlantic and returned to tell about the vast sea and world beyond, the ancients took down the mythical *Ne plus ultra* spanning the Strait of Gibraltar and put up another mythical scroll reading, *Plus ultra*—"More beyond."

For centuries, mankind had despaired that the grave was the end. But with the resurrection of Jesus Christ, hope was born in the hearts of men and women facing death. Because of His resurrection and ascension into heaven, mankind's *Ne plus ultra* has been changed to God's *Plus ultra*—"More beyond."

Sacrifice

One of the great historic sites in Texas is the Alamo in San Antonio. On February 23, 1836, Mexican General Santa Anna and more than four thousand troops attacked the Alamo.

The Alamo was defended by only 182 freedom-loving men. Among them were James Bowie, William Travis, and Davy Crockett.

When the smoke of battle had cleared, only eight defenders remained alive, and these were promptly shot. According to some authorities, the only ones to survive the hideous massacre were a Mrs. Dickinson, her baby, her Mexican nurse, and a black boy.

Texas has placed a memorial plaque upon the wall of the Alamo to those who sacrificed their lives there for Texas freedom. The plaque reads:

> It was here that a gallant few, the bravest of the brave, threw themselves between the enemy and the settlements, determined never to surrender nor retreat. They redeemed their pledge to Texas with a forfeit of their lives. They fell the chosen sacrifice to Texas freedom.

Just as the freedom of Texas was born out of sacrifice, so the freedom believers have in Jesus Christ comes from His sacrifice upon the cross.

Security

Oliver Cromwell ruled England from 1649-1658 during the period of the Commonwealth and Protectorate. Born in Huntingdon in 1599, Cromwell died in 1658. He was a man of high moral purpose.

Oliver Cromwell loved the passage from Deuteronomy 33:27, "Underneath are the everlasting arms."

He had these words framed, then hung them above his bed. They were a constant reminder from which he drew fresh strength and courage for the responsibilities that were his.

The words paint a beautiful picture. When the eaglet got old enough to try its wings, the mother eagle destroyed the nest, forcing the little bird out. Then taking the eaglet on her broad back, the mother eagle would soar high above the trees and hills. Flying high above the mountain crags and trees, she would tilt her wings just a little, and the eaglet would slide off into the rare air of the high places.

Fluttering, screaming, the eaglet would drift downward, coaxing its little wings to work. All the while, the mother would circle around it, assuring it that she was near and that all would be well.

When the little bird was about to crash onto the rocks below, the strong, skillful mother would glide under the eaglet, catch it on her back, and soar to the heights again.

Then, flying high toward the sun, they would repeat the same process until the eaglet had learned to fly.

But during those attempts to fly, the mother bird was there— "underneath [were] the everlasting arms."

Self

Almost every boy and girl in America has heard the story of a little girl who fell down a rabbit hole and discovered a marvelous land of adventure. Also, she drank a magic potion and ate magic cake, and at times she was only three-inches tall. Her name was Alice, and she lived in Wonderland. She talked to a caterpillar, watched a baby turn into a pig, and had a tea party with a March Hare.

The book, as you know, was the story of *Alice in Wonderland*, and it was written by Lewis Carroll.

In another one of Carroll's magical and wonderful stories for children, he told about a padlock. It was just an ordinary padlock, except it was alive. It had long, thin arms and legs and was always very nervous, running here and there.

One day, another character in the story stopped the twisting, turning, wiggling padlock and asked, "What is the matter with you? Why are you so excited and unhappy?"

Waving his thin arms wildly in the air, the padlock exclaimed, "I am seeking the key to unlock myself!"

Is there such a key that will help one come to grips with himself or herself? The Christian gospel says there is, and that key is Jesus Christ.

Sorrow

Mary Ann Evans was her real name. But she wrote under the pen name George Eliot. All schoolchildren will eventually meet George Eliot as they read her novels *Silas Marner* and *The Mill on the Floss*.

During a particularly difficult time in her life, George Eliot wrote to a close friend, "My address is Grief Castle."

All of us sooner or later will live at that address, for sorrow is our common legacy.

Soul

Clarence Darrow was an outstanding American criminal lawyer.

Born in Ohio in 1857, he died in 1938. Perhaps Darrow's most famous case was the John T. Scopes "Monkey Trial" in 1925 in Dayton, Tennessee. Defending the right to teach evolution in the Tennessee public schools, Darrow was opposed by William Jennings Bryan.

Darrow lived to be nearly eighty-one, but in his seventy-eighth year and near the end of his days, Darrow wrote: "All my life, I have been seeking proof of God, something I could put my finger on and say, 'This is a fact.' But my doubts are at rest. I know that such fact does not exist. When I die, as I shall soon, my body will decay, my mind will decay and my intellect will be gone. My soul? There is no such thing."

Strength

One of the twentieth-century's great Christian leaders was Martin Niemöller. Niemöller was a Jewish Christian who survived Adolf Hitler's Dachau prison during World War II. He died in Weisbaden on March 6, 1984, at the age of ninety-two.

Niemöller took a stand against Hitler. As a result, he was arrested and thrown into solitary confinement. Every day, the stench of burning human flesh and the sight of walking dead men haunted him.

When the war ended, Niemöller came to the United States. Once, as he was being interviewed by a Chicago radio station, he was asked how he could stand Dachau and solitary confinement without losing his sanity.

He replied that one doesn't know how much one can suffer until the test comes. But one can stand far more than one thinks, he declared.

"If God is dwelling in your life," he said, "you can stand far more than you think."

Success

Nathaniel Hawthorne, described by English poet Edward Fitzgerald as "the most of a man of genius America has produced in the way of imagination," neither succeeded quickly nor easily. For much of his life, Hawthorne lived in obscurity.

Although he had produced *Twice-Told Tales*, Hawthorne still could not live from the meager money he made selling his writings. To tide him over, he accepted a position in the Salem Custom House where he was paid $1,200 a year.

But the political wind out of Washington changed, and Hawthorne was dismissed. A shifting of those political winds brought him back to the custom house. They shifted again, and he was put out.

But Hawthorne's trying experience in the custom house was really a blessing in disguise. It gave him a rich background from which he wrote *The Scarlett Letter*, and through it he gained immediate recognition.

At Bowdoin College, Hawthorne excelled in English composition. But in other subjects, he was only an average student. When he graduated in 1825, he was determined to become a writer.

Then came the quiet years in which Hawthorne matured. For the next ten years, he learned his craft and read widely. He worked at various jobs to keep body and soul together. Editing schoolbooks, doing farm work, and working in both the Boston and Salem custom houses helped prepare Hawthorne.

But it was not until 1850, twenty-five years after Hawthorne finished college, that he won fame with *The Scarlet Letter*.

Success in any endeavor usually does not come easily. Dedication to one's day-by-day tasks is the key that unlocks that door.

Sufficient

General William Booth, an English Methodist minister, founded the Salvation Army in London in 1878. Emma, his second daughter, married a man by the name of Tucker, who also worked for the Salvation Army.

One day Tucker preached in Chicago on the sufficiency of Jesus to comfort in every situation. After the service, a working man cornered Tucker and told him that it was easy for Tucker to talk about the comfort and grace of Jesus because Tucker's wife was still alive.

The man told Tucker that he had lost his wife and that his babies were crying for their mother who would never return. He then told Tucker that if he had that kind of sorrow, he might not speak so glowingly of Christ's sufficiency.

It wasn't very long until Tucker lost his wife in a railroad accident, and her body was brought back to Chicago's Salvation Army headquarters for the funeral service.

As Tucker looked at his silent wife, he thought of what the sorrowing man had said to him a few days earlier.

Addressing those who had come for the funeral service, Tucker looked around for the man but did not see him. He then told the mourners that if the man were there, he wanted him to know that Christ was sufficient for his motherless children and his grieving heart.

Unknown to Tucker, the man was there. He came down the aisle, knelt beside the casket, and received Tucker's Savior for himself.

When Nansen, the great Arctic explorer, was looking for the North Pole, his ship drifted one day into very deep water. Needing to know the water's depth, Nansen let down the sounding line to calculate. When he had played out all the line that he had on board the ship, and still he had not reached the bottom of the ocean, he noted in his logbook: "35,000 fathoms and deeper than that."

If our faith falters before some locked door or some great opportunity or some heart-breaking sorrow, we may find ourselves asking, "Is God's grace enough for this?"

Be still and listen, and you will hear the answer echoing back to you from some saint who has walked that way before you.

"Yes," that voice will whisper, "and greater than that!"

Trials

Sometimes the most severe weather produces the most beautiful flowers.

Thomas Edison, history's greatest inventor, confessed that his near deafness was a great asset to his concentration.

John Milton's blindness produced his immortal *Paradise Lost*.

George Matheson's disappointment produced one of our greatest Christian hymns, "O Love That Wilt Not Let Me Go."

John Bunyan's imprisonment in Bedford's jail gave him time to write one of history's most-read books, *The Pilgrim's Progress*.

Marco Polo's yearlong imprisonment gave him time to put down on paper his explorations of Asia. Titled *The Book of Marco Polo*, it laid open the mystical land of Asia to European eyes.

Beethoven's deafness fell on him when he was only forty-two, but in his silent world, he produced some of history's most stirring music.

Joseph's tragic life—sold into slavery as a teenager—enabled him to become the savior of his people.

Phillips Brooks, one of America's early and magnificent preachers, wanted to teach school, but he was never able to make the grades, so he turned to preaching.

James Whistler, who immortalized his mother in his famous painting, was thrown out of West Point because he appeared one day for roll call dressed only in his socks. General Robert E. Lee dismissed him, but it was the making of Whistler.

Booker T. Washington, born in slavery, became the greatest educator of his race. Often, he spoke of "the advantages of disadvantages."

Blind and deaf, Helen Keller inspired the world with her determination.

Sir Walter Scott, perhaps best known for "Ivanhoe," wanted to be a poet, but he was always eclipsed by George Gordon

Byron. Rather than giving up, he turned to the novel, where he found himself and fame.

William Cowper, melancholic and suicidal, overcame his emotional problems to write "There Is a Fountain Filled with Blood" and "God Moves in a Mysterious Way His Wonders to Perform."

Unbelief

Sometime before the turn of the century, United Brethren Church Bishop Wright spoke at a college in the Midwest.

Addressing the students, the bishop pompously declared, "Everything that can be invented has already been invented."

Later, the president of the college suggested to the bishop that perhaps there were still some things to be invented. But the bishop stood his ground.

"Name me one thing," the bishop snorted.

"I believe someday men will build a machine that will fly in the air," the president replied.

"That is the most stupid idea I have ever heard," the bishop answered. "If God had wanted man to fly, He would have given him wings."

Bishop Wright had two sons. One of them was named Orville, and the other was named Wilbur. On December 17, 1903, they proved their father wrong when they made the world's first flight in a power-driven machine at Kitty Hawk, North Carolina.

Unbelief always locks doors to opportunity and blinds eyes to possibilities.

But unbelief's final sting is much worse. It locks people out from the grace of God, the thing they most desperately need.

And it, alone, condemns a sinner to hell.[†]

Universe

This vast and complex universe is a testimony to the creative and sustaining power of God.

Starlight travels at 186,000 miles per second. In a year, starlight will travel 6 trillion miles. But our galaxy alone is so immense that if we could travel at the speed of light, it would take us more than 20,000 light years to travel through the center of it. It would take 100,000 light years to travel from one side of it to the other.

The earth spins through space like a spaceship. Every twenty-four hours, the earth makes a complete revolution, and it is always traveling eastward. Traveling at the rate of 1,100 miles a minute, it takes the earth 365 and one-fouth days to make one orbit around the sun. Every year, our spaceship Earth travels 600 million miles through space.

The earth is not round, it is oblique—flattened at the two poles. That is why the diameter of the equator is twenty-six miles longer than the diameter from pole to pole. The diameter at the equator is 7,926 miles, but the diameter at the poles is 7,900 miles. Whereas the diameter of the earth at the equator is 7,926 miles, the diameter of the moon is 2,160 miles. But the diameter of the sun is 865,370 miles.

Compared to the earth, the sun is 110 times larger. One million earths could be stuffed into the interior of the sun. If the earth were the size of a green pea and the sun the size of a beach ball, they would need to be separated 130 feet to correspond to the relationship between them.

Although there may be as many as one hundred billion stars in our galaxy, we can only see about six thousand of them from the earth. And the sun is one of those stars. The star nearest the earth is 25 trillion miles away from us—four light years. Rigel, a star in the Orion group, is one of the brightest stars in our heavens. Rigel's light travels to the earth at 186,000 miles per second, but it takes it 500 years to reach us. Shining gloriously in the heavens 1,800 times brighter than the sun, the light from Rigel that we will see tonight left Rigel about the time Columbus discovered America.

Well did the psalmist describe God's glory in this universe when he said, "The heavens declare the glory of God" (Ps. 19:1).

In the late 1950s, the world's most complicated clock was put on display in the town hall of Copenhagen, Denmark. It took forty years to build the clock, and it cost more than $1 million. It has ten faces and contains fifteen thousand parts.

The clock not only tells the time, but it also tells the days of the week, the month, and the year. It tells about the movement of the planets and is able to calculate the position of the stars for the next twenty-five thousand years. And doing all of this, it is so accurate that it will neither lose nor gain more than two fifths of a second in a three-hundred-year period.

How do we know that the clock is so accurate and dependable? Because it has been set by the universe itself. And that universe, timed by the touch of God, runs on schedule.

Victory

The line that separates defeat from victory is often a very fine line. Frequently, just one more effort will bring victory when defeat seems almost certain.

For example, during the Civil War, Union General Ulysses S. Grant sent orders to General Philip Sheridan to destroy the Confederate forces at Winchester, Virginia.

When Sheridan rode in among his troops, the bluecoats were retreating. Riding at full gallop, waving his sword above his head, and pointing it toward the Confederate lines, Sheridan shouted, "Turn, boys, turn! We're going back!"

Following their fearless leader, the Yankess turned, charged the Confederate lines, and won a smashing victory.

War

C. E. Montague was on the editorial staff of England's *Manchester Guardian* when World War I broke out. Eager to save democracy, Montague tried to enlist in the army. But his hair was turning gray, and Montague was refused. Dying his hair, Montague applied at another recruiting station and was accepted.

When it came time for Montague to ship out, his colleagues on the paper saluted him with a toast. Admitting that they had heard of men and women's hair turning white overnight because of cowardice, they confessed Montague was the only man they knew whose hair had turned dark overnight because of courage.

Montague saw what war was like, and then he saw the kind of peace that came out of the war. One by one, the things for which he had sacrificed collapsed in the postwar era.

So Montague wrote a book about his experiences, and he called it *Disenchantment*.

About the most disenchanting and pointless thing man ever invented was war. There are winners, but there are no victors.

Wealth

Patrick Henry knew that material riches are not the only form of wealth.

Speaking before the Virginia Provencial Convention in 1775, Henry urged the Virginia militia to arm itself against England. In that speech, he spoke the immortal words: "Give me liberty, or give me death!"

When Patrick Henry drew up his last will and testament, he included this as the closing paragraph: "I have now disposed of all my property to my family; there is one thing more I wish I could give thee, and that is the Christian religion. If they had this, and I had not given them one shilling, they would be rich: And if they had not this, and I had given them the whole world, they would still be poor."

The wealth that lasts—our spiritual assets—cannot be counted in dollars and cents.

Work

Few are born with silver spoons in their mouths. Most people who succeed do so not because they are brilliant but because they work harder than the next person.

Demosthenes became history's greatest orator, but it wasn't easy. As a young man, he fought against a speech impediment. But through hard work, he overcame it.

William Cowper, the Englishman who wrote our moving hymn "There Is a Fountain Filled with Blood," had a long-running battle with melancholy. And several times, he tried to commit suicide. But determination and hard work paid off, and Cowper lived to bless the lives of millions.

And what about Napoleon? Whatever one may think about his genius or lack of it, he brought Europe to her knees. But he didn't do it because he was brilliant. Out of the forty-three young men who graduated in his military class, Napoleon was number forty-two.

Thomas Edison, history's greatest inventor, had a lifelong battle with near deafness. Robert Louis Stevenson, the Scottish poet and novelist, struggled with tuberculosis. And Helen Keller, a blessing to millions, was handicapped by both blindness and deafness.

Sir Walter Scott was plagued by lameness. Benjamin Disraeli, the only Jew ever elected prime minister of Great Britain, fought a lifelong battle against prejudice. Abraham Lincoln had the double odds of poverty and a lack of education working against him.

Lou Gehrig, perhaps the greatest baseball player in the history of the game,, didn't have an easy go of it, either. He was forever playing with broken bones in his hands, but that didn't stop Gehrig.

In one way or the other, each of us has a handicap. The odds are stacked against us. And if we are going to succeed against those odds, which sometimes are formidable, we are going to have to work to do it.

Generally speaking, the harder we work at it, the more we succeed.

Worry

In his book *Living All Your Life*, author John A. Redhead tells about a Bishop Quayle. Tired but unable to sleep, Quayle turned and tossed in his bed, fretting over problems he could not solve.

The bishop said that suddenly, someone walked into his room unannounced, and Quayle recognized that it was God.

When asked what was the reason for his sleeplessness, the bishop confessed that he was worried over a certain matter.

Addressing the bishop, God said, "Quayle, you go to sleep, and I'll sit up the rest of the night."

Perhaps it was the bishop's quaint way of telling us that we ought to cast all of our problems upon Jesus, because He cares for us.

When Abraham Lincoln was a young country lawyer, he and several lawyer friends frequently rode the circuit to try cases.

On one of those circuit-riding trips, he and his friends encountered drenching downpours and flooded creeks and rivers. And they were anxious about going on.

They were most concerned about Fox River, for it was the most dangerous of all the rivers in that area to cross when it was flooding.

Encountering a circuit-riding Methodist preacher who knew all the rivers and creeks in the area, they asked him about crossing Fox River. And he answered that he had often crossed it and knew all about it.

But, the preacher confessed, "I have one fixed rule with regard to Fox River: I never cross it till I reach it."

This is what Jesus was saying about fretting today over tomorrow's problems (Matt. 6:25-34).[†]

Topical Index

148

Polo, Marco
Scott, Sir Walter
Washington, Booker T.
Whistler, James

Unbelief . . . .   Wright, Bishop
Wright, Orville
Wright, Wilbur

Victory . . . .   Grant, Gen. Ulysses S.
Sheridan, Gen. Philip

War . . . .   Montague, C. E.
Wealth . . . .   Henry, Patrick
Work . . . .   Cowper, William
Demosthenes
Disraeli, Benjamin
Edison, Thomas
Gehrig, Lou
Keller, Helen
Lincoln, Abraham
Napoleon
Scott, Sir Walter
Stevenson, Robert Louis
Worry . . . .   Lincoln, Abraham
Quayle, Bishop
Redhead, John A.

Alphabetical Index

154